D1712989

WINTER

WINTER

by

Dallas Lore Sharp

illustrated by

Robert Bruce Horsfall

YESTERDAY'S CLASSICS

ITHACA, NEW YORK

This edition, first published in 2017 by Yesterday's Classics, an imprint of Yesterday's Classics, LLC, is an unabridged republication of the text originally published by Houghton Mifflin Company in 1912. For the complete listing of the books that are published by Yesterday's Classics, please visit www.yesterdaysclassics. com. Yesterday's Classics is the publishing arm of the Baldwin Online Children's Literature Project which presents the complete text of hundreds of classic books for children at www.mainlesson.com.

ISBN: 978-1-63334-022-0

Yesterday's Classics, LLC
PO Box 339
Ithaca, NY 14851

CONTENTS

CHAPTER I

HUNTING THE SNOW

YOU want no gun, no club, no game-bag, no steel trap, no snare when you go hunting the snow. Rubber boots or overshoes, a good, stout stick to help you up the ridges, a pair of field-glasses and a keen eye, are all you need for this hunt,—besides, of course, the snow and the open country.

You have shoveled the first snow of the winter; you have been snowballing in it; you have coasted on it; and gone sleigh-riding over it; but unless you have gone hunting over it you have missed the rarest, best sport that the first snowfall can bring you.

Of all the days to be out in the woods, the day that follows the first snowfall is—the best? No, not the best. For there is the day in April when you go after arbutus; and there is the day in June when the turtles come out to lay in the sand; the muggy, cloudy day in August when the perch are hungry for you in the creek; the hazy Indian Summer day when the chestnuts are dropping for you in the pastures; the keen, crisp February day when the ice spreads glassy-clear and smooth for you over the mill-pond; the muddy, raw, half-thawed, half-lighted, half-drowned March day when the pussy-willows are

1

breaking, and the first spring frogs are piping to you from the meadow. Then there is—every day, every one of the three hundred and sixty-five days, each of them best days to be out in the live world of the fields and woods.

But one of the very best days to be out in the woods is the day that follows the first winter snowfall, for that is the day when you must shoulder a good stout stick and go gunning. Gunning with a stick? Yes, with a stick, and rubber boots, and bird-glasses. Along with this outfit you might take a small jointed foot-rule with which to measure your quarry, and a notebook to carry the game home in.

It ought to be the day after the first real snow, but not if that snow happens to be a blizzard and lies deep in dry powdery drifts, for then you could hardly follow a trail if you should find one. Do not try the hunt, either, if the snow comes heavy and wet; for then the animals will stay in their dens until the snow melts, knowing, as they do, that the soft slushy stuff will soon disappear. The snow you need will lie even and smooth, an inch or two deep, and will be just damp enough to pack into tight snowballs.

If, however, the early snows are not ideal, then wait until over an old crusted snow there falls a fresh layer about an inch deep. This may prove even better hunting, for by this time in the winter the animals and birds are quite used to snow-walking, and besides, their stores of food are now running short, compelling them to venture forth whether or not they wish to go.

It was early in December that our first hunting-snow came last year. We were ready for it, waiting for it, and when the winter sun broke over the ridge, we started the hunt at the hen-yard gate, where we saw tracks in the thin, new snow that led us up the ridge, and along its narrow back, to a hollow stump. Here

the hunt began in earnest; for not until that trail of close, double, nail-pointed prints went under the stump were the four small boys convinced that we were tracking a skunk and not a cat.

The creature had moved leisurely—that you could tell by the closeness of the prints. Wide-apart tracks in the snow mean hurry. Now a cat, going as slowly as this creature went, would have put down her dainty feet almost in a single line, and would have left round, cushion-marked holes[1] in the snow, not triangular, nail-

---

[1] *cushion-marked holes:* Examine a cat's feet. Make a study of cat tracks: how they are placed; how wide apart; how they look when she walks, when she runs, when she jumps, when she gathers herself together for a spring. You can learn the art of snow-hunting by studying the tracks of the cat in your own dooryards.

pointed prints like these. Cats do not venture into holes under stumps, either.

We had bagged our first quarry! No, no! We had not pulled that wood pussy[2] out of his hole and put him into our game-bag. We did not want to do that. We really carried no bag; and if we had, we should not have put the wood pussy into it, for we were hunting tracks, not animals, and "bagging our quarry" meant trailing a creature to its den, or following its track till we had discovered something it had done, or what its business was, and why it was out. We were on the snow for animal *facts*, not pelts.[3]

We were elated with our luck, for this stump was not five minutes by the ridge path from the hen-yard. And here, standing on the stump, we were only sixty

[2]*wood pussy:* a polite name in New England for the skunk.

[3]Study the drawings of the tracks in this chapter, then go into the woods and try to identify the tracks you find in the snow. Every track you discover and identify will be quarry in your bag—just as truly as though you had killed a deer or a moose or a bear. You can all turn snow-hunters without leaving blood and pain and death and emptiness and silence behind you. And it is just as good and exciting sport.

minutes away from Boston Common by the automobile, driving no faster than the law allows. So we were hunting, not in a wilderness, but just outside our dooryard and almost within the borders of a great city.

And that is the first interesting fact of our morning hunt. No one but a lover of the woods and a careful walker on the snow would believe that here in the midst of hayfields, in sight of the smoke of city factories, so many of the original wild wood-folk still live and travel their night paths undisturbed.

Still, this is a rather rough bit of country, broken, ledgy, boulder-strewn, with swamps and woody hills that alternate with small towns and cultivated fields for many miles around.

Here the animals are still at home, as this hole of the skunk's under the stump proved. But there was more proof. As we topped the ridge on the trail of the skunk, we crossed another trail, made up of bunches of four prints,—two long and broad, two small and roundish,—spaced about a yard apart.

A hundred times, the winter before, we had tried that trail in the hope of finding the form or the burrow of its maker; but it crossed and turned and doubled, and always led us into a tangle, out of which we never got a clue. It was the track of the great northern hare,[4] as we knew, and we were relieved to see the strong prints of our cunning neighbor again; for, what with the foxes

---

[4]*the great northern hare:* The northern hare is not often seen here, and I am not sure but that this may be the common brown rabbit.

5

and the hunters, we were afraid it might have fared ill with him. But here he was, with four good legs under him; and, after bagging our skunk, we returned to pick up the hare's trail, to try our luck once more.

We followed his long, leisurely leaps down the ridge, out into our mowing-field, and over to the birches below the house. Here he had capered about in the snow, had stood up on his haunches and gnawed the bark from off a green oak sucker two and a half feet from the ground. This, doubtless, was pretty near his length, stretched out—an interesting item; not exact to the inch, perhaps, but close enough for us; for who would care to kill him in order to measure him with scientific accuracy?

Nor was this all; for up the footpath through the birches came the marks of two dogs. They joined the marks of the hare. And then, back along the edge of the woods to the bushy ridge, we saw a pretty race.

It was all in our imaginations, all done for us by those long-flinging footprints in the snow. But we saw it all—the white hare, the yelling hounds, nip and tuck,

in a burst of speed across the open field which must have left a gap in the wind behind.

It had all come as a surprise. The hounds had climbed the hill on the scent of a fox, and had started the hare unexpectedly. Off he had gone with a jump.

But just such a jump of fear is what a hare's magnificent legs were intended for.

Those legs carried him a clear twelve feet in some of the longest leaps for the ridge; and they carried him to safety, so far as we could read the snow. In the medley of hare-and-hound tracks on the ridge there was no sign of a tragedy. He had escaped again—but how and where we have still to learn.

We had bagged our hare,—yet we have him still to bag,—and taking up the trail of one of the dogs, we continued our hunt. One of the joys of this snow hunting is having a definite road or trail blazed for you by knowing, purposeful wild-animal feet.

You do not have to blunder ahead breaking your way into this wilderness world, trusting luck to bring you somewhere. The wild animal or the dog goes this way, and not that, for a reason. You are watching that reason all along; you are pack-fellow to the hound; you hunt with him.

Here the hound had thrust his muzzle into a snowcapped pile of slashings,[5] had gone clear round the pile, then continued on his way. But we stopped; for out of the pile, in a single, direct line, ran a number of mouse prints, going and coming. A dozen white-footed mice might have traveled that road since the day before, when the snow had ceased falling.

We entered the tiny road, for in this kind of hunting a mouse is as good as a mink, and found ourselves descending the woods toward the garden patch below. Halfway down we came to a great red oak, into a hole at the base of which, as into the portal of some mighty castle, ran the road of the mice. That was the end of it. There was not a single straying footprint beyond the tree.

I reached in as far as my arm would go, and drew out a fistful of pop-corn cobs. So here was part of my scanty crop! I pushed in again, and gathered up a bunch of chestnut shells, hickory-nuts and several neatly rifled hazelnuts.[6] This was story enough. There must

---

[5]*slashings:* The name for the waste limbs and tops left after cutting forest trees. Tree wardens should compel the woodchoppers to pile this brush up as they cut, and burn it while the snow is on the ground to prevent forest fires in summer.

[6]*hazelnuts:* small brown nuts like the filberts of the stores. They grow on a bush two to six feet high. There are two kinds,—common hazelnut and beaked hazelnut. The green

be a family of mice living
under the slashing-
pile, who for some
good reason kept
their stores here in
the recesses of this
ancient red oak. Or was this some
squirrel's barn being pilfered by the
mice, as my barn is the year round? It
was not all plain. But this question, this
constant riddle of the woods, is part of our
constant joy in the woods. Life is always new,
and always strange, and always fascinating.

It has all been studied and classified
according to species. Any one knowing the
woods at all, would know that these were
mouse tracks, would even know that they
were the tracks of the white-footed mouse,
and not the tracks of the jumping mouse,
the house mouse, or the meadow mouse.
But what is the whole small story of these
prints? What purpose, what intention, what
feeling, do they spell? What and why?—a
hundred times!

So it is not the bare tracks that we are
hunting; it is the meaning of the tracks—
where they are going, and what they are going

husk looks like a cap, hence its Saxon name *haesle*, a cap, and
the scientific name *Corylus* from the Greek *corys*, a helmet.

9

for. Burns[7] saw a little mouse run across the furrows as he was plowing and wrote a poem about it. So could we write a poem if we like Burns would stop to think what the running of these little mice across the snow might mean. The woods and fields, summer and winter, are full of poems that might be written if we only knew just all that the tiny snow-prints of a wood mouse mean, or understood just what, "root and all, and all in all,"[8] the humblest flower is.

The pop-corn cobs, however, we did understand; they told a plain story; and, falling in with a gray squirrel's track not far from the red oak, we went on, our burdenless game-bag heavier, our hearts lighter that we, by the sweat of our brows, had contributed a few ears of corn to the comfort of this snowy winter world.

The squirrel's track wound up and down the hillside, wove in and out and round and round, hitting every possible tree, as if the only road for a squirrel was one that looped and doubled, and tied up every stump, and zigzagged into every tree trunk in the woods.

But all this maze was no ordinary journey. He had not run this coil of a road for breakfast, because a squirrel, when he travels, say for distant nuts, goes as directly as you go to your school or office; only he goes not by streets, but by trees, never crossing more of the

[7]*Burns:* Robert Burns, the Scotch poet.

[8]*root and all, and all in all:* from a poem by Lord Tennyson called "Flower in the Crannied Wall."

open in a single rush than the space between him and the nearest tree that will take him on his way.

What interested us here in the woods was the fact that a second series of tracks, just like the first, except that they were only about half as large, dogged the larger tracks persistently, leaping tree for tree, and landing track for track with astonishing accuracy—tracks which, had they not been evidently those of a smaller squirrel, would have read to us most menacingly.

As this was the mating season for squirrels, I suggested that it might have been a kind of Atalanta's race[9] here in the woods. But why did so little a squirrel want to mate with one so large? They would not look well together, was the answer of the small boys. They thought it much more likely that Father Squirrel had been playing wood-tag with one of his children.

Then, suddenly, as sometimes happens in the woods, the true meaning of the signs was fairly hurled at us, for down the hill, squealing and panting, rushed a full-

[9]*Atalanta's race:* Look up the story of the beautiful girl runner who lost her race with her lover because of her desire to pick up a golden apple

sized gray squirrel, with a red squirrel like a shadow, like a weasel, at his heels.

For just an instant I thought it was a weasel, so swift and silent and gliding were its movements, so set and cruel seemed its expression, so sure, so inevitable, its victory.

Whether it ever caught the gray squirrel or not, and what it would have done had it caught the big fellow, I do not know. But I have seen the chase often—the gray squirrel nearly exhausted with fright and fatigue, the red squirrel hard after him. They tore round and round us, then up over the hill, and disappeared.

One of the rarest prints for most snow-hunters nowadays, but one of the commonest hereabouts, is the

quick, sharp track of the fox. In the spring particularly, when my fancy young chickens are turned out to pasture, I have spells of fearing that the fox will never be exterminated here in this untillable but beautiful chicken country. In the winter, however, when I see Reynard's trail across my lawn, when I hear the music of the baying hounds and catch a glimpse of the white-tipped brush swinging serenely in advance of the coming pack, I cannot but admire the capable, cunning rascal, cannot but be glad for him, and marvel at him, so resourceful, so superior to his almost impossible conditions, his almost numberless foes.

We started across the meadow on his trail, but found it leading so straightaway for the ledges, and so continuously blotted out by the passing of the pack, that, striking the wallowy path of a muskrat in the middle of the meadow, we took up the new scent to see what the shuffling, cowering water-rat wanted from across the snow.

A man is known by the company he keeps, by the way he wears his hat, by the manner of his laugh; and among the wild animals nothing tells more of character than their manner of moving. You can read animal character as easily in the snow as you can read act and direction.

The timidity, the indecision, the lack of purpose, the restless, meaningless curiosity of this muskrat were evident from the first in the starting, stopping, returning, going-on track he had plowed out in the thin snow.

He did not know where he was going or what he was going for; he knew only that he insisted upon going back, but all the while kept going on; that he wanted to go to the right or to the left, yet kept moving straight ahead.

We came to a big wallow in the snow, where, in sudden fear, he had had a fit at the thought of something that might not have happened to him had he stayed at home. Every foot of the trail read, "He would if he could; if he couldn't, how could he?"

We followed him on, across a dozen other trails, for it is not every winter night that the muskrat's feet get the better of his head, and, willy-nilly, take him abroad. Strange and fatal weakness! He goes

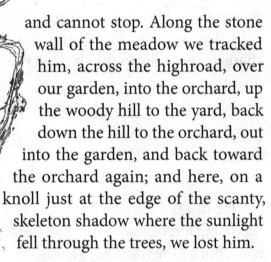

and cannot stop. Along the stone wall of the meadow we tracked him, across the highroad, over our garden, into the orchard, up the woody hill to the yard, back down the hill to the orchard, out into the garden, and back toward the orchard again; and here, on a knoll just at the edge of the scanty, skeleton shadow where the sunlight fell through the trees, we lost him.

Two mighty wings,[10] we saw, had touched the snow lightly here, and the lumbering trail had vanished as into the air.

Close and mysterious the shadowy silent wings hang poised indoors and out. Laughter and tears are

[10] *Two mighty wings:* an owl's wing marks, perhaps the barred owl or the great horned owl, or the snowy owl, which sometimes comes down from the north in the winter.

companions. Life begins, but death sometimes ends the trail. Yet the sum of life, outdoors and in, is peace, gladness, and fulfillment.

CHAPTER II

THE TURKEY DRIVE

THE situation was serious enough for the two boys. It was not a large fortune, but it was their whole fortune, that straggled along the slushy road in the shape of five hundred weary, hungry turkeys, which were looking for a roosting-place.

But there was no place where they could roost, no safe place, as the boys well knew, for on each side of the old road stretched the forest trees, a dangerous, and in the weakened condition of the turkeys, an impossible roost on such a night as was coming.

For the warm south wind had again veered to the north; the slush was beginning to grow crusty, and a fine sifting of snow was slanting through the open trees. Although it was still early afternoon, the gloom of the night had already settled over the forest, and the turkeys, with empty crops, were peevishly searching the bare trees for a roost.

It was a strange, slow procession that they made, here in the New Brunswick forest—the flock of five hundred turkeys, toled forward by a boy of eighteen, kept in line by a well-trained shepherd-dog[11] that raced up and down the straggling column, and urged on in the rear by a boy of nineteen, who was followed, in his turn, by an old horse and farm wagon, creeping along behind.

It was growing more difficult all the time to keep the turkeys moving. But they must not be allowed to stop until darkness should put an end to the march. And they must not be allowed to take to the trees at all. Some of them, indeed, were too weak to roost high; but the flock would never move forward again if exposed in the tall trees on such a night as this promised to be.

The thing to do was to keep them stirring. Once allow them to halt, give one of them time to pick out a roosting-limb for himself, and the march would be over for that afternoon. The boys knew their flock. This was not their first drive. They knew from experience that once a turkey gets it into his small head to roost, he is bound to roost. Nothing will stop him. And in this matter the flock acts as a single bird.

In the last village, back along the road, through which they had passed, this very flock took a notion suddenly to go to roost, and to go to roost on a little chapel as the vesper bells were tolling. The bells were tolling, the worshipers were gathering, when, with a loud gobble, one of the turkeys in the flock sailed into the air and alighted upon the ridgepole beside the belfry! Instantly the flock broke ranks, ran wildly round

---

[11]*shepherd-dog:* Only a well-trained dog would do, for turkeys are very timid and greatly afraid of a strange dog.

the little building, and with a clamor that drowned the vesper bell, came down on the chapel in a feathered congregation that covered every shingle of the roof. Only the humor and quick wit of the kindly old priest prevented the superstitious of his people from going into a panic. The service had to wait until the birds made themselves comfortable for the night—belfry, roof, window-sills, and porch steps thick with roosting turkeys!

The boys had come to have almost a fear of this mania for roosting, for they never knew when it might break out or what strange turn it might take. They knew now, as the snow and the gray dusk began to thicken in the woods, that the flock must not go to roost. Even the dog understood the signs,—the peevish *quint, quint, quint,* the sudden bolting of some gobbler into the brush, the stretching necks, the lagging steps,—and redoubled his efforts to keep the line from halting.

For two days the flock had been without food. Almost a week's supply of grain, enough to carry them through to the border, had been loaded into the wagon before starting in upon this wild, deserted road through the Black Creek[12] region; but the heavy, day-long snowstorm had prevented their moving at all for one day, and had made travel so nearly impossible since then that here they were, facing a blizzard, with night upon them, five hundred starving turkeys straggling wearily before them, and a two days' drive yet to go!

The two brothers had got a short leave from college,

[12]*Black Creek:* a local name; not in the Geography.

and had started their turkey drive in the more settled regions back from the New Brunswick border. They had bought up the turkeys from farm to farm, had herded them in one great flock as they drove them leisurely along, and had moved all the while toward the state line, whence they planned to send them through Maine for the New England market. Upon reaching the railroad, they would rest and feed the birds, and ship them, in a special freight-car ordered in advance, to a Boston commission house, sell the horse and rig for what they could get, and, with their dog, go directly back to college.

More money than they actually possessed had gone into the daring venture. But the drive had been more than successful until the beginning of the Black Creek road. The year before they had gone over the same route, which they had chosen because it was sparsely settled and because the prices were low. This year the farmers were expecting them; the turkeys were plentiful; and the traveling had been good until this early snow had caught them here in the backwoods and held them; and now, with the sudden shift of the wind again to the north, it threatened to delay them farther, past all chance of bringing a single turkey through alive.

But George and Herbert Totman had not worked their way into their junior year at college to sit down by the roadside while there was light to travel by. They were not the kind to let their turkeys go to roost before sundown. It was a slow and solemn procession that moved through the woods, but it moved—toward a goal that they had set for that day's travel.

All day, at long intervals, as they had pushed along the deep forest road, the muffled rumble of distant trains had come to them through the silence; and now, although neither of them had mentioned it, they were determined to get out somewhere near the tracks before the night and the storm should settle down upon them. Their road, hardly more here than a wide trail, must cross the railroad tracks, as they remembered it, not more than two or three miles ahead.

Leaving more and more of the desolate forest behind them with every step, they plodded doggedly on. But there was so much of the same desolate forest still before them! Yet yonder, and not far away, was the narrow path of the iron track through the interminable waste; something human—the very sight of it enough to warm and cheer them. They would camp to-night where they could see a train go by.

The leaden sky lowered closer upon them. The storm had not yet got under full headway, but the fine icy flakes were flying faster, slanting farther, and the wind was beginning to drone through the trees.

Without a halt, the flock moved on through the thickening storm. But the dog was having all that he could do to keep the stragglers in order; and George, in the rear, saw that they must stir the flock, for the birds were gradually falling back into a thick bunch before him.

Hurrying back to the wagon, he got two loaves of bread, and ran ahead with them to Herbert. The famished turkeys seemed to know what he carried, and broke into a run after him. For half a mile they kept up the gait, as both boys, trotting along the road, dropped pieces of bread on the snow.

Then the whole game had to be repeated; for the greater part of the flock, falling hopelessly behind, soon forgot what they were running after, and began to cry, *"Quint! quint! quint!"*—the roosting-cry! So, starting again in the rear with the bread, George carried the last of the flock forward for another good run.

"We should win this game," Herbert panted, "if we only had loaves enough to make a few more touch-downs."

"There's half an hour yet to play," was George's answer.

"But what on?"

"Oh, on our nerve now," the older boy replied grimly.

"That railroad is not far ahead," said Herbert.

"Half an hour ahead. We've got to camp by that track to-night or—"

"Or what?"

But George had turned to help the dog head off some runaways.

Herbert, picking up a lump of frozen leaves and snow, began to break this in front of the flock to tole them on.

He had hardly started the birds again, when a long-legged gobbler brushed past him and went swinging down the road, calling, *"Quint! quint! quint!"* to the flock behind. The call was taken up and passed along the now extended line, which, breaking immediately into double-quick, went streaming after him.

Herbert got out of the way to let them pass, too astonished for a moment to do more than watch them go. It was the roosting-cry! An old gobbler had given it; but as it was taking him, for once, in the right direction, Herbert ordered back the dog that had dashed forward to head him off, and fell in with George to help on the stragglers in the rear.

As the laggards were brought up to a slight rise in the road, the flock was seen a hundred yards ahead, gathered in a dark mass about a telegraph-pole! It could be nothing else, for through the whirling snow the big cross-arms stood out, dim but unmistakable.

It was this that the gobbler had spied and started for, this sawed and squared piece of timber, that had suggested a barnyard to him,—corn and roost,—as to the boys it meant a human presence in the forest and something like human companionship.

It was after four o'clock now, and the night was hard upon them. The wind was strengthening every minute; the snow was coming finer and swifter. The boys' worst fears about the storm were beginning to be realized.

But the sight of the railroad track heartened them. The strong-armed poles, with their humming wires, reached out hands of hope to them; and getting among the turkeys, they began to hurry them off the track and down the steep embankment, which fortunately offered them here some slight protection from the wind. But as fast as they pushed the birds off, the one-minded things came back on the track. The whole flock, meanwhile, was scattering up and down the iron rails and settling calmly down upon them for the night.

They were going to roost upon the track! The railroad bank shelved down to the woods on each side, and along its whitened peak lay the two black rails like ridge-poles along the length of a long roof. In the thick half-light of the whirling snow, the turkeys seemed suddenly to find themselves at home: and as close together as they could crowd, with their breasts all to the storm, they arranged themselves in two long lines upon the steel rails.

And nothing could move them! As fast as one was tossed down the bank, up he came. Starting down the lines, the boys pushed and shoved to clear the track; but the lines re-formed behind them quickly, evenly, and almost without a sound. As well try to sweep back the waves of the sea! They worked together to collect a small band of the birds and drive them into the edge of the woods; but every time the band dwindled to a single turkey that dodged between their legs toward its place on the roost. The two boys could have kept *two* turkeys off the rails, but not five hundred.

"The game is up, George," said Herbert, as the sickening thought of a passing train swept over him.

The words were hardly uttered when there came the *tankle, tankle* of the big cow-bell hanging from the collar of the horse, that was just now coming up to the crossing!

George caught his breath and started over to stop the horse, when, above the loud hum of the wires and the sound of the wind in the forest trees, they heard through the storm the muffled whistle of a locomotive.

"Quick! The horse, Herbert! Hitch him to a tree and come!" called George, as he dived into the wagon and pulled out their lantern. "Those birds could wreck the train!" he shouted, and hurried forward along the track with his lighted lantern in his hand.

It was not the thought of the turkeys, but the thought of the people on the flying Montreal express,—if that it was,—that sped him up the track. In his imagination he saw the wreck of a ditched train below him; the moans of a hundred mangled beings he heard sounding in his ears!

On into the teeth of the blinding storm he raced, while he strained his eyes for a glimpse of the coming train.

The track seemed to lie straightaway in front of him, and he bent his head for a moment before the wind, when, out of the smother of the snow, the flaring headlight leaped almost upon him.

He sprang aside, stumbled, and pitched headlong down the bank, as the engine of a freight, with a roar that dazed him, swept past.

But the engineer had seen him, and there was a screaming of iron brakes, a crashing of cars together, and a long-drawn shrieking of wheels, as the heavy train slid along the slippery rails to a stop.

As the engineer swung down from his cab, he was met, to his great astonishment, by a dozen turkeys clambering up the embankment toward him. He had plowed his way well among the roosting flock and brushed them unhurt from the rails as the engine skidded along to its slow stop.

By this time the conductor and the train-hands had run forward to see what it all meant, and stood looking at the strange obstruction on the track, when Herbert came into the glare of the headlight and joined them. Then George came panting up, and the boys tried to explain the situation. But their explanation only made a case of sheer negligence out of what at first had seemed a mystery to the trainmen. Both the engineer and the conductor were anxious and surly. Their train was already an hour late; there was a through express behind, and the track must be cleared at once.

And they fell at once to clearing it—conductor, fireman, brakemen, and the two boys. Those railroad men had never tried to clear a track of roosting turkeys before. They cleared it,—a little of it,—but it would not stay cleared, for the turkeys slipped through their hands, squeezed between their legs, ducked about their heels, and got back into place. Finally the conductor, putting two men in line on each rail, ordered the engineer to follow slowly, close upon their heels, with the train, as they scattered the birds before them.

The boys had not once thought of themselves. They

had had no time to think of anything but the danger and the delay that they had caused. They helped with all their might to get the train through, and as they worked, silently listened to the repeated threats of the conductor.

At last, with a muttered something, the conductor kicked one of the turkeys into a fluttering heap beneath the engine, and, turning, commanded his crew to stand aside and let the engineer finish the rest of the flock.

The men got away from the track. Then, catching Herbert by the arm, George pointed along the train, and bending, made a tossing motion toward the top of the cars.

"Quick!" he whispered. "One on every car!" and stepping calmly back in front of the engine, he went down the opposite side of the long train.

As he passed the tender, he seized a big gobbler, and sent him with a wild throw up to the top of a low coal-car, just as Herbert, on his side, sent another fluttering up to the same perch. Both birds landed with a flap and a gobble that were heard by the other turkeys up and down the length of the train.

Instantly came a chorus of answering gobbles[13] as every turkey along the track saw, in the failing light, that real buildings—farmyard buildings—were here to roost on! And into the air they went, helped all along the train by the two boys, who were tossing them into

[13] *a chorus of answering gobbles:* Turkeys will follow their leader. It was this habit or trait that the boys now made use of.

26

the cars, or upon the loads of lumber, as fast as they could pass from car to car.

Luckily, the rails were sleety, and the mighty driving-wheels, spinning on the ice with their long load, which seemed to freeze continually to the track, made headway so slowly that the whole flock had come to roost upon the cars before the train was fairly moving.

Conductor and brakeman, hurrying back to board the caboose, were midway of the train before they noticed what was happening. *How* it was happening they did not see at all, so hidden were the movements of the two boys in the swirl of the blinding snow.

For just an instant the conductor checked himself. But it was too late to do anything. The train was moving, and he must keep it moving as fast as he could to the freight-yards ahead at the junction—the very yards where, even now, an empty car was waiting for the overdue turkeys.

As he ran on down the track and swung aboard the

caboose, two other figures closed in behind the train. One of them, seizing the other by the arm, landed him safe upon the steps, and then shouted at him through the storm:—

"Certainly you shall! I'm safe enough! I'll drive on to that old sawmill to-night. Feed 'em in the morning and wait for me! Good-by," and as the wind carried his voice away, George Totman found himself staring after a ghost-white car that had vanished in the storm.

He was alone; but the thought of the great flock speeding on to the town ahead was company enough. Besides, he had too much to do, and to do quickly, to think of himself; for the snow was blocking his road, and the cold was getting at him. But how the wires overhead sang to him! How the sounding forest sang to him as he went back to give the horse a snatch of supper!

He was soon on the road, where the wind at his back and the tall trees gave him protection. The four-wheeled wagon pulled hard through the piling snow, but the horse had had an easy day, and George kept him going until, toward eight o'clock, he drew up behind a lofty pile of slabs and sawdust at the old mill.

A wilder storm never filled the resounding forests of the North. The old mill was far from being proof against the fine, icy snow; but when George rolled himself in his heavy blanket and lay down beside his dog, it was to go to sleep to the comfortable munching of the horse, and with the thought that Herbert and the turkeys were safe.

And they were safe. It was late in the afternoon the next day when George, having left the wagon at the mill, came floundering behind the horse through the unbroken road into the streets of the junction, to find Herbert anxiously waiting for him, and the turkeys, with full crops, trying hard to go to roost inside their double-decked car.

CHAPTER III

WHITE-FOOT

THE December rain was falling down, down, down, as if the drops were lead instead of water. The December sky, if you could call it sky, had settled down, down, down, as if it too were of lead, and were being propped up only by the tops of the stiff bare trees.

A green stick in the fireplace behind me sizzled and sputtered and blew its small steam whistles to warn me away from the window,—from the sight of the naked trees, and the cold, thick fog upon the meadow, and the blur of the pine woods beyond, and the rain falling down, down, down.

A dreary world out of doors surely, with not a sign of life! The pine tree, rising up above the hillside in front of the window, was green, but only a few lifeless leaves rattled among the middle branches of the oaks, while up in the stark top of a hickory sapling was wedged a robin's nest, deserted and wet and going to pieces.

I shivered, in spite of the hearth-fire behind me, for the face of the gray gloom pressed close up against the window outside. And the empty robin's nest, already a ruin! its mud walls broken, its tiny timbers hanging loose in the rain!

But what a large nest for a robin, I thought; and how strangely peaked and pointed it is, like a little haycock! Then all at once, inside of me, and all over me, I felt a warm, delightful feeling.

"It isn't possible," said I aloud, but all to myself; "it isn't possible that little White-Foot[14] has moved into that old robin's nest and fitted it up with a peaked roof for the winter?"

And the thought of it started the warm, delightful feeling again inside of me and all over me; and snatching up the tongs by the fireplace I ran out into the December rain and tapped a few times on the slender hickory sapling.

And what do you think happened?

It stopped raining?

No.

You broke your tongs?

No.

The nest fell out and hit you on the head?

No.

You ran back into the house again out of the rain?

Yes, I did, and I went straight to the window and looked out again at the robin's nest,—my deserted,

---

[14] *White-Foot:* the deer, or wood mouse *(Peromyscus leucopus).*

ruined robin's nest, with its thick thatch of waterproof cedar bark, with its little round door-hole in the side, with its soft furry bed, all toasty warm, out of which with my tapping tongs I had just roused White-Foot and brought him sleepy-eyed to look down at me from his door.

The rain continued to fall down; but my spirits went up, and up, at the thought of that little mouse all safe and warm for the winter in Robin's deserted nest.

And so, if "there are no birds in last year's nest,"[15] as mourns a doleful poem, you need not be sad on that account, for if you look closely, you may find, now and then, a mouse in last year's nest—and who will say that finding a mouse in a bird's nest is not almost as interesting as finding a bird there?

A robin's nest in the winter-time would be the wettest, muddiest, coldest place in the world for a robin; but a mouse can take that old robin's nest and turn it into a snuggery (if you know what a "snuggery" is) so cozy and warm that neither the tip of Mr. Mouse's sharp nose, nor the tip of his thin ears, nor the tippy-tip of his long bare tail ever feels one sharp nip of the cold outside.

So, if there are no birds in last year's nest (as surely there ought not to be), take your tongs and tap, or, better, climb up, and reach gently into the nest with your finger, for a mouse may be waiting inside to bite you,—and that would be interesting.

[15] *"there are no birds in last year's nest"*: a line from a poem by Longfellow called "It is not always May."

For a mouse is interesting—just as interesting in his mousy ways as a whale in his whalish ways, or a robin in his ways. Can you name anything that does not grow interesting as soon as you begin to watch and study it? Large things, small things, Bengal tigers or earthworms—all things will surprise and interest you if you will study them for a season.

I have a friend, for instance, who has shot more tigers, in more lands, than any other living man; who knows more about tiger habits and the tempers of the dangerous beasts than any other man; and who, as I am writing this, is himself writing a book which is to be called *Tiger Lands*. That will be an exciting book, no doubt, for he has had adventures that made my hair stand up on my head, just to hear about. Yet I very much doubt if that book, with all its man-eaters, will be any more interesting or any more valuable to us than Darwin's book on earthworms.[16]

So am I going to sigh because there are no birds in last year's nests? Had the poem said, "there are no *mice* in last year's nests," that might have made me sad, perhaps; though I am sure that I could go into the woods almost any winter day and find plenty of old *stumps* with mice in them. And I am equally sure that there will be plenty of birds in next summer's nests; so, until the robins come back and build new nests, I am going to look out of the window these dark December days, and think of White-Foot in Robin's old nest, high up there in the slender sapling, where no cat can climb

[16]*Darwin's book on earthworms:* Read in this book how the worms make garden soil.

to him, and where no crow will dare come to tear his house to pieces.

There he will swing in the winter gales with the snow swirling around and beneath him; there he will dream through the rain and the slanting sleet when his high sapling stairway is coated with ice and impossible for him to climb; there he will live, and whenever I thump with the tongs at his outer gate, up there in the little round doorway will appear his head—his eyes, I should say, for he looks all eyes up there, so large, so black, so innocent, so inquiring are they, so near to rolling off down the tip of his nose with sheer surprise.

I shall have many a cheering glimpse of White-Foot, many a comforting thought of him, out there, his thatch snow-covered, his thick-walled nest in the slender hickory riding the winter seas that sweep the hilltop, as safe as the ships anchored yonder in the landlocked harbor; and he will be much more comforting to me out there than here in the house with me; for, strangely enough, while White-Foot never seems to join the common mice in the barn, never a winter goes by without one or more of his kind coming into the house for the cold weather.

This would be very pleasant if they could keep out of the pop-corn and the nuts and the apples and the linen-drawers. But only recently one got into the linen in the china-closet, and chewed together the loveliest damask nest that any being ever slept in.

There was nothing for such conduct, then, of course, except to kill her. But I did not kill her, though I take

THERE HE WILL SWING IN THE WINTER GALES

no credit to myself, for I tried to kill her, as any one would have been tempted to do.

I got her out of that linen-drawer in a hurry and chased her from cupboard to couch, to radiator and bookcase, and lost her. The next day I resumed the chase, and upset most of the furniture before she finally gave me the slip. The next day she appeared, and once more we turned things upside down, and once more from some safe corner she watched me put the chairs back on their legs and pick up the pieces of things.

But the next morning, as I opened the grate of the kitchen stove to light the fire, there in the ash-pan huddled that little mouse; and  under her in a bed of ashes, as if to reproach me forever, were five wee mice, just born, blind and naked in the choking dust, babes that should have been sleeping covered in a bed of downy damask in the linen-drawer.

I said I did not kill her. No, I reached in slowly, lifted her and her babes out softly in my hand, carried them into a safe, warm place and left them, devoutly hoping that they might all grow up to help themselves, if need be, to an ear of pop-corn, or even to a cozy corner and a sip of honey in the beehives.

No, I don't believe I hoped all of that, for White-Foot is exceedingly fond of honey, and no roof in all the out-of-doors is so much to his liking as a beehive, warm with the heat of the clustered swarm; and nowhere can he make such a nuisance of himself as inside the hive.

A robin's nest, a beehive, a linen-drawer, a wood-pecker's hole—almost any place will do for the winter home, so thick and warm can the mice build their walls, so many bins of acorns and grain do they lay up, and so bold are they to forage when their winter stores run low.

I had a curious experience with a white-footed mouse in the cellar one winter. The small boys had carried into the cellar (to hide them from me, I imagine) about four quarts of chestnuts which they had gathered. A little later, when they went to get their nuts, the box was empty. Not a chestnut left!

"Have you eaten all our chestnuts, father?"

"No, I haven't—not a nut," I answered.

"Well, they are all gone!" was the wail.

And so they were, but how, and where, we did not know. House mice had not eaten them, for no shells were left behind; there were no rats or squirrels in the cellar that fall; and as for one of the small boys—that was past thought. The fact is, more suspicion was attached to me in the case than anything in my previous conduct called for; and, though altogether guiltless, I continued to be uncomfortably quizzed from time to time about those chestnuts, until I began to wonder if I *had* got up in my sleep and devoured the four quarts, shells and all.

Then one day, while we were putting things shipshape in the vegetable cellar, what did we come upon but a nice little pile of chestnuts hidden away in a dark corner; then we discovered another pile, laid up carefully, neatly, in a secret spot, where no human eye—except the human house-cleaning eye, that misses nothing—would ever have seen them, and where no big human hand would ever have put them.

I was allowed to go then and there scot-free; and a trap was set for the wood mouse. It was White-Foot, we knew. But we never caught her. And I am glad of it, for after we took away what chestnuts we could find, she evidently felt it necessary to make a new hoard, and began with a handful of old hickory-nuts, shagbarks, that had been left in the vegetable cellar beside the box of chestnuts.

Now, however, she felt the insecurity of the inner cellar, or else she had found a fine big bin out in the furnace cellar, for out there by the furnace she took those nuts and tucked them compactly away into the toe of one of my tall hunting-boots.

There were double doors and a brick partition wall between the two cellars. No matter. Here were the nuts she had not yet stored; and out yonder was the hole, smooth and deep and dark, to store them in. She found a way past the partition wall.

Every morning I shook those nuts out of my boot and sent them rattling over the cellar floor. Every night the mouse gathered them up and put them snugly back into the toe of the boot. She could not have carried more than one nut at a time—up the tall boot-leg and down the oily, slippery inside.

I should have liked to see her scurrying about the cellar, looking after her curiously difficult harvest. Apparently, they were new nuts to her every evening. Once I came down to find them lying untouched. The mouse, perhaps, was away over night on other business. But the following morning they were all gathered and nicely packed in the boot as before. And as before I sent them sixty ways among the barrels and boxes of the furnace room.

But I did it once too often, for it dawned upon the mouse one night that these were the same old nuts that she had gathered now a dozen times. That night they disappeared. Where? I wondered.

Weeks passed, and I had entirely forgotten about the nuts, when I came upon them, the identical nuts of my boot, tiered carefully up in a corner of the deep, empty water-tank away off in the attic!

CHAPTER IV

A CHAPTER OF THINGS TO SEE THIS WINTER

I

THE first snowstorm! I would not miss seeing the first snowstorm, not if I had to climb up to my high, tarry, smoky roof in the city and lie down on my back, as I once did, in order to shut out everything but the gray wavering flakes that came scattering from the sky. But how marvelously white and airy they looked, too, coming down over the blackened city of roofs, transfiguring it with their floating veil of purity! You must see the first snowfall, and, if you want to, jump and caper with the flakes, as I always do.

II

The sorrows of winter are its storms. They are its greatest glories also. One should no more miss the sight of the winter storms than he should miss the sight of the winter birds and stars, the winter suns and moons! A storm in summer is only an incident; in winter it is an event, a part of the main design. Nature gives herself over by the month to the planning and bringing off of the winter storms—vast arctic shows, the dreams of her wildest moods, the work of her mightiest minions. Do not miss the soft feathery fall that plumes the trees and that roofs the sheds with Carrara marble; the howling blizzard with its fine cutting blast that whirls into smoking crests; the ice-storm that comes as slow, soft rain to freeze as it falls, turning all the world to crystal: these are some of the miracles of winter that you must not fail to see.

III

You must see how close you had passed to and fro all summer to the vireo's nest, hanging from the fork on

a branch of some low bush or tree, so near to the path that it almost brushed your hat. Yet you never saw it!

Go on and make a study of the empty nests; see

particularly how many of them were built out along the roads or paths, as if the builders wished to be near their human neighbors—as, indeed, I believe they do. Study how the different birds build—materials, shapes, finish, supports; for winter is the better season in which to make such study, the summer being so crowded with interests of its own.

IV

When the snow hardens, especially after a strong wind, go out to see what you can find in the wind furrows of the snow—in the holes, hollows, pockets, and in footprints in the snow. Nothing? Look again, closely—that dust—wind-sweepings—seeds!

Yes, seeds. Gather several small boxes of them and when you return home take a small magnifying glass and make them out—the sticktights, gray birches, yellow birches, pines, ragweeds, milfoil—I cannot number them! It is a lesson in the way the winds and the snows help to plant the earth. Last winter I followed for some distance the deep frozen tracks of a fox, picking out the various seeds that had drifted into every footprint, just so far apart, as if planted in the snow by some modern planting-machine. It was very interesting.

V

When the snow lies five or six inches deep, walk out along the fence-rows, roadsides, and old fields to see the juncos, the sparrows, and goldfinches feeding upon the seeds of the dead weeds standing stiff and brown above the snow. Does the sight mean anything to you? What does it mean?

VI

Burns has a fine poem beginning—

> "When biting Boreas, fell and doure,
> Sharp shivers thro' the leafless bow'r,"

in which, he asks,—

> "Ilk happing bird—wee, helpless thing!—
> · · · · · · · ·
> What comes o' thee?
> Whare wilt thou cow'r thy chittering wing,
> An' close thy e'e?"

43

Did you ever ask yourself the question? Go forth, then, as the dusk begins to fall one of these chill winter days and try to see "what comes o'" the birds, where they sleep these winter nights. You will find an account of my own watching in a chapter called "Birds' Winter Beds" in *Wild Life Near Home.*

VII

You will come back from your watching in the dusk with the feeling that a winter night for the birds is unspeakably dreary, perilous, and chill. You will close the door on the darkness outside with a shiver as much from dread as from the cold.

"List'ning the doors an' winnocks rattle,"—

you will think of the partridge beneath the snow, the crow in his swaying pine-top, the kinglet in the close-armed cedar, the wild duck riding out the storm in his freezing water-hole, and you will be glad for your four thick walls and downy blankets, and you will wonder how any creature can live through the long, long night of cold and dark and storm. But there is another view of this same picture; another picture, rather, of this same stormy, bitter night which you must not miss seeing. Go out to see how the animals sleep, what beds they have, what covers to keep off the cold: the mice in the corn-shocks; the muskrats in their thick mud homes; the red squirrels in their rocking, wind-swung beds, so soft with cedar bark and so warm that never a tooth of the cold can bite through!

> "I heard nae mair, for Chanticleer
> Shook off the pouthery snaw,
> And hail'd the morning with a cheer,
> A cottage-rousing craw."

VIII

This winter I have had two letters asking me how best to study the mosses and lichens, and I answered, "Begin now." Winter, when the leaves are off, the ground bare, the birds and flowers gone, and all is reduced to singleness and simplicity—winter is the time to observe the shapes, colors, varieties, and growth of the lichens. Not that every lover of nature needs to know the long Latin names (and many of these lesser plants have no other names), but that every lover of the out-of-doors should notice them—the part they play in the color of things, the place they hold in the scheme of things, their exquisite shapes and strange habits.

IX

You should see the brook, "bordered with sparkling frost-work . . . as gay as with its fringe of summer flowers." You should examine under a microscope the wonderful crystal form of the snowflakes—each flake shaped by an infinitely accurate hand according to a pattern that seems the perfection, the very poetry, of mechanical drawing.

X

What a world of gray days, waste lands, bare woods, and frozen waters there is to see! And you should see them—gray and bare and waste and frozen. But what is a frozen pond for if not to be skated on? and waste white lands, but to go sleighing over? and cold gray days, but so many opportunities to stay indoors with your good books?

See the winter bleak and cheerless as at times you will, and as at times you ought; still if you will look twice, and think as you look, you will see the fishermen on the ponds catching pickerel through the ice—life swimming there under the frozen surface! You will see the bare empty woodland fresh budded to the tip of each tiny twig—life all over the trees thrust forward to catch the touch of spring! You will see the wide flinty fields thick sown with seeds—life, more life than the sun and the soil can feed, sleeping there under "the tender, sculpturesque, immaculate, warming, fertilizing snow"![17]

---

[17]Here are ten different things for you to see this winter, and most of them, whether you live in the city or country, you can see, provided you live where the snow falls. But you will have some kind of a winter no matter where you live. Don't miss it—its storms, its birds, its animals, its coasting, skating, snowshoeing, its invitations to tramp the frozen marshes and deep swamps where you cannot go in the summer, and where, on the snow, you will catch many a glimpse of wild life that the rank summer sedges will never reveal. Don't stop with these ten suggestions; there are a hundred other interesting things to see. And as you see them, write about them.

CHAPTER V

CHRISTMAS IN THE WOODS

> " 'Twas the night before Christmas,
> and all through the house
> Not a creature was stirring,
> not even a mouse."[18]

B UT on the night before this particular Christmas every creature of the woods that could stir was up and stirring; for over the old snow was falling swiftly, silently, a soft, fresh covering that might mean a hungry Christmas unless the dinner were had before morning.

Yet, when the morning dawned, a cheery Christmas sun broke across the great gum swamp,[19] lighting the snowy boles and soft-piled limbs of the giant trees with indescribable glory, and pouring, a golden flood, into the deep, spongy bottom of the swamp below. It would be a perfect Christmas in the woods, clear, mild, stirless,

[18]These lines of poetry you all know. But who can tell who wrote them? Where did he live and when?

[19]*gum swamp:* See description of such a swamp on pages 262-263 of the author's *Wild Life Near Home.* This is the tree known as sour gum, more properly tupelo (*Nyssa sylvatica* or *uniflora*).

with silent footing for me, and everywhere the telltale snow.

And everywhere in the woods would be the Christmas spirit, too. As I paused among the pointed cedars of the pasture, looking down into the tangle at the head of the swamp, a clear, wild whistle rang in the thicket, followed by a flash through the alders like a tongue of fire, as a cardinal grosbeak[20] shot down to the tangle of greenbrier and magnolia under the slope of the hill. The bird was a fleck of flaming summer. As warm as summer, too, were the pointed cones of stag-horn sumac burning on the crest of the ridge against the group of holly trees—trees as fresh as April, and all aglow with red berries.

The woods were decorated for the Holy Day.[21] The gentleness of the soft, new snow touched everything; cheer and good-will lighted the unclouded sky and warmed the thick depths of the evergreens, and blazed in the crimson-berried bushes of the ilex[22] and the alder. The Christmas woods were glad. The heart of the woods was full of Christmas peace.

Now I did not imagine all of this as I went along. Perhaps there was the spirit of Christmas in my heart, and so I found the spirit of Christmas in the woods;

[20]*cardinal grosbeak:* Commonly called "cardinal," or "redbird."

[21]*Holy Day:* What was the oldest form of our word "holiday"?

[22]*ilex: Ilex verticillata,* the black alder, or winterberry, one of the holly family. A low swamp bush covered with red berries all winter.

but so it must have been with the household I had just left, back on the city street. Every one had Christmas in his heart, and so every one found Christmas in the Christmas-tree blazing and glittering in its candle-flame blossoms and jeweled fruit.

So there was real Christmas joy and peace—a real Christmas spirit—abroad in the woods this snowy Christmas morning. The sky had it, the trees had it, the soft white slopes had it, the softly flowing creek had it, flowing softly toward the bay.

But doubtless my own feelings had something to do with it all. This was Christmas Day, and these were my home woods, the woods where I tramped and trapped and "grew up" when a boy; and this was I, after twenty years of absence, I, the boy again, back in the old familiar pasture on my way to Lupton's Pond![23]

Yes, I must say that I was almost afraid as I followed the old cow-path across the pasture, now only a slightly sunken line in the snow; I was afraid that the path might be gone. Twenty years are a good many years for a cow-path to last. But evidently the cows had been crossing every year since I had been away; and not a single new crook had they worn in the old winding trail. Then I was afraid, as I came to the fence where I could look down upon the pond, lest the pond might have disappeared. But no, there it lay, sealed over, as if kept for me by the snow! Then I looked fearfully over the pond, over the

[23] *Lupton's Pond:* A little pond along Cohansey Creek near Bridgeton, N. J.

steep ridge on the opposite shore to where there used to stand two particular persimmon trees.[24]

My heart beat wildly for a moment. The woods up the ridge had been cut off! Things had changed! I was confused and looked this way and that, when, so near to me that I could scarcely believe my eyes, I saw the twin trees, their hard, angular limbs closely globed with fruit, and standing softly out against the sky!

It was enough. Forgetting the twenty years, I hurried down across the pond and up to the persimmon trees on the other side—up into the trees indeed, for I never stopped until I had climbed clear up into the top among the ripe persimmons!

Do you know what a persimmon, picked from a particular tree along Cohansey Creek on Christmas Day, tastes like? especially when you have not had a taste of persimmon for twenty years? No, you do not—because you are not twenty years old, perhaps, and because you were not a boy along Cohansey Creek, perhaps, and because, if you were, you did not know those two particular persimmon trees, maybe.

Nobody ever seemed to know the perfection of those persimmons, except myself and the 'possums. Not one of the Luptons, who owned the pasture, the pond, and the trees, had ever been a boy, so far as I could remember, and certainly not one of them had ever tasted the fruit of those two trees. There were other persimmon trees up and down the township, others

[24]*Persimmon trees:* found from New Haven, Conn., to Florida.

here along the pond; but these two were the only trees to hold their fruit until Christmas, preserved with such richness of flavor, such a gummy, candied, wild, woodsy quality, that it could not decay. Those persimmons never decayed. They candied, evaporated, wrinkled, fell, and vanished away.

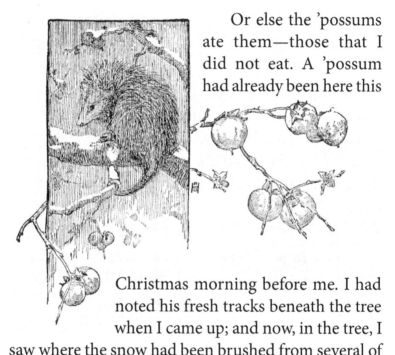

Or else the 'possums ate them—those that I did not eat. A 'possum had already been here this Christmas morning before me. I had noted his fresh tracks beneath the tree when I came up; and now, in the tree, I saw where the snow had been brushed from several of the large limbs as the 'possum had moved about in the top, eating his Christmas dinner.

You never ate a Christmas dinner high up in the top of a persimmon tree? But you will, perhaps, some day, as good a Christmas dinner, I hope, as ours was. For such persimmons! Bob Cratchit's goose ("There never was such a goose!")[25] could not have been any better

[25] *Bob Cratchit's goose:* There never was such a goose, as you all know who have read Dickens's *Christmas Carol.*

flavored. Nor could the little Cratchits have been any hungrier for goose than I was for persimmons.

Now the 'possum had been having persimmons every night since the frosts of October; so of course he felt no such hunger for persimmons as I felt. But ripe persimmons would be a Christmas dinner for a 'possum every day in the year. There is nothing so unspeakably good as persimmons if you happen to be a 'possum, or if you happen to be a boy—even after twenty years!

So the 'possum and I had our Christmas dinner together at Nature's invitation, in the top of the persimmon tree. The 'possum, to be sure, had eaten and gone before I came. But that is good form in the woods. He was expecting me, so he came early, just before dawn, that neither of us might be embarrassed, leaving his greetings for me in sign-language in the snow.

A Christmas dinner all alone would be cold cheer indeed. But I was not alone. Here was good company and plenty of it. Did not the tracks talk to me? With abundance of fruit still left in the tree, did I need to see that 'possum fold up his napkin, pull down his vest, spread his hands over his expansive person and groan in the fullness of his feast? No; all of that was printed plainly in the snow. Why, I could even hear his groans in his tumbled tracks at the foot of the tree, where the fat old fellow had literally fallen over himself! What an appetite! What a pudding of persimmons he must be! He can hardly walk for fat! Look at his trail in the snow leading down toward the pond—a big wide wallow where he has bounced along!

So I slide down the tree and take up the 'possum's trail. We have broken bread together, this 'possum and I, and now we will enter the woods together in the same good-fellowship for the rest of the day. Persimmons and good-will are very proper things to be filled with when you go into the Christmas woods.

And there is no better fellowship for such a tramp than the trail of some animal like the 'possum or the mink or the fox. To go in with one of these through the woods-door is to find yourself at home. Any one can manage to get inside the woods, as the grocery boy or the census man manages to get inside our houses. You can bolt in at any time on business. But a trail, remember, is Nature's invitation. Go softly in with 'possum, or rabbit, or coon, and at the threshold of the trees you will be met by the Spirit of the Woods—you will be made a guest in this secret, shadowy house of the out-of-doors.

But do not fail first to break bread with the 'possum. A persimmon, or a handful of wintergreen berries, or a nip of sassafras root, or a piece of spruce gum, or a lump of liquid amber[26]—share anything, take any small part in the life of these who live wild in the woods, and they will meet you at the threshold and make you more than welcome.

I went in with the 'possum. He had traveled home leisurely and without fear, as his tracks plainly showed.

[26]*liquid amber:* The balsamic juice of the sweet gum tree, sometimes called "bilsted" (*Liquidambar styraciflua*), a large, beautiful swamp tree found from Connecticut to Florida and west to Texas.

He was full of persimmons. A good happy world this, where such fare could be had for the picking! What need to hurry home? Unless, indeed, one were in danger of falling asleep by the way! So I thought, too, as I followed his winding path; and if I was tracking him to his den, it was only to wake him for a moment with the compliments of the season. But when I finally found him in his hollow gum, he was so sound asleep he barely knew that some one was poking him gently in the ribs and wishing him a merry Christmas.

The 'possum had led me far along the creek to the centre of the empty, hollow swamp, where the great-boled gums lifted their branches like a timbered, unshingled roof between me and the wide sky. Far away through the spaces of the rafters I saw a pair of wheeling buzzards, and under them, in lesser circles, a broad-winged hawk. Here, at the feet of the tall, clean trees, looking up through the leafless limbs, I had something of a measure for the flight of the great birds. And what power, what majesty and mystery in those distant buoyant wings!

I have seen the turkey buzzard sailing the skies on the bitterest winter days. To-day, however, could hardly be called winter. Indeed, nothing yet had felt the pinch of the cold. There was no hunger yet in the swamp, though this new snow had scared the raccoons out, and their half-human tracks[27] along the margin of

---

[27]*half-human tracks:* Because the coon is a relative of the bears and has a long hind foot that leaves a track much like that of a small baby.

the swamp stream showed that, if not hungry, they at least feared that they might be.

For a coon hates snow. He invariably stays in during the first light snowfalls, and even in the late winter he will not venture forth in fresh snow unless driven by hunger or some other dire need. Perhaps, like a cat or a hen, he dislikes the wetting of his feet. Or it may be that the soft snow makes bad hunting—for him. The truth is, I believe, that such a snow makes too good hunting for the dogs and the gunner. The new snow tells too clear a story. For the coon's home is no dark den among the ledges; only a hollow in some ancient oak or tupelo.[28] Once within, he is safe from the dogs, but his long, fierce fight for life taught him generations ago that the nest-tree is a fatal trap when behind the dogs come the axe and the gun. So he has grown wary and enduring. He waits until the snow grows crusty, when without sign, and almost without scent, he can slip forth among the long shadows and prowl to the edge of dawn.

Skirting the stream out toward the higher back woods, I chanced to spy a bunch of snow in one of the great sour gums,[29] that I thought was an old nest. A second look showed me tiny green leaves, then white berries, then mistletoe!

It was not a surprise, however, for I had found it here before—a long, long time before. It was back in my schoolboy days that I first stood here under the

[28]*tupelo:* See note on gum swamp, page 47.

[29]*sour gums:* same as tupelo.

mistletoe and had my first romance. There was no chandelier, no pretty girl, in that romance—only a boy, the mistletoe, the giant trees, and the sombre silent swamp. But there was more than that, there was the thrill of discovery, for until that day the boy did not know that mistletoe grew outside of England, did not know that it grew in his own native swamps! Rambling alone through the swamps along the creek that day, he stopped under a big curious bunch of green, high up in one of the gums, and—made his first discovery!

So this Christmas Day the boy climbed up again at the peril of his precious neck, and brought down a bit of that old romance.

I followed the stream along through the swamp to the open meadows, and then on under the steep wooded hillside that ran up to the higher land of corn and melon fields. Here at the foot of the slope the winter sun lay warm, and here in the sheltered, briery border I came upon the Christmas birds.

There was a great variety of them, feeding and preening and chirping in the vines. The tangle was a-twitter with their quiet, cheery talk. Such a medley of notes you could not hear at any other season outside a city bird store. How far the different species understood one another I should like to know, and whether the hum of voices meant sociability to them, as it certainly did to me. Doubtless the first cause of their flocking here was the sheltered warmth and the great numbers of berry-laden bushes, for there was no lack of abundance or of variety on this Christmas table.

In sight from where I stood hung bunches of withering chicken, or frost, grapes,[30] plump clusters of blue-black berries of the greenbrier, and limbs of the smooth winterberry[31] beaded with their flaming fruit. There were bushes of crimson ilex, too, trees of fruiting dogwood and holly, cedars in berry, dwarf sumac and seedy sedges, while patches on the wood slopes uncovered by the sun were spread with trailing partridge-berry and the coral-fruited wintergreen. I had eaten part of my dinner with the 'possum; now I picked a quantity of these wintergreen berries, and continued my meal with the birds. And they too, like the 'possum, had enough, and to spare.

Among the birds in the tangle was a large flock of northern fox sparrows,[32] whose vigorous and continuous scratching in the bared spots made a most lively and cheery commotion.

Many of them were splashing about in tiny pools of snow-water, melted partly by the sun and partly by the warmth of their bodies as they bathed. One would

[30] *chicken or frost grapes: Vitis cordifolia:* the smallest, sourest, best (boy standards) of all our wild grapes. They ripen *after* the frost and feed the boys and birds when all other such fruits have gone from the woods.

[31] *smooth winterberry:* is really another ilex, *Ilex lavigata,* a larger bush than *Ilex verticillata,* the black alder or winterberry.

[32] *fox sparrows:* See the picture on the next page. The largest, most beautiful of our sparrows. Nests in the Far North. A migrant to New England and the Southern States.

THE FOX SPARROWS' BATH

hop to a softening bit of snow at the base of a tussock, keel over and begin to flop, soon sending up a shower of sparkling drops from his rather chilly tub. A winter snow-water bath seemed a necessity, a luxury indeed; for they all indulged, splashing with the same purpose and zest that they put into their scratching among the leaves.

A much bigger splashing drew me quietly through the bushes to find a marsh hawk giving himself a Christmas souse. The scratching, washing, and talking of the birds; the masses of green in the cedars, holly, and laurels; the glowing colors of the berries against the snow; the blue of the sky, and the golden warmth of the light made Christmas in the heart of the noon, that the very swamp seemed to feel.

Two months later there was to be scant picking here, for this was the beginning of the severest winter I ever knew. From this very ridge, in February, I had reports of berries gone, of birds starving, of whole coveys of quail frozen dead in the snow; but neither the birds nor I dreamed to-day of any such hunger and death. A flock of robins whirled into the cedars above me; a pair of cardinals whistled back and forth; tree sparrows, juncos, nuthatches, chickadees, and cedar-birds cheeped among the trees and bushes; and from the farm lands at the top of the slope rang the calls of meadowlarks.

Halfway up the hill I stopped under a blackjack oak, where, in the thin snow, there were signs of something like a Christmas revel. The ground was sprinkled with acorn-shells and trampled over with feet of several kinds and sizes,—quail, jay, and partridge feet; rabbit, squirrel, and mouse feet, all over the snow as the feast of acorns had gone on. Hundreds of the acorns were lying about, gnawed away at the cup end, where the shell was thinnest, many of them further broken and cleaned out by the birds.

As I sat studying the signs in the snow, my eye caught a tiny trail leading out from the others straight away toward a broken pile of cord-wood. The tracks were planted one after the other, so directly in line as to seem like the prints of a single foot. "That's a weasel's trail," I said, "the death's-head at this feast," and followed it slowly to the pile of wood. A shiver crept over me as I felt, even sooner than I saw, a pair of small, sinister eyes fixed upon mine. The evil pointed head, heavy but

alert, and with a suggestion of fierce strength out of all proportion to the slender body, was watching me from between the sticks of cord-wood. And just so had it been watching the mice and the rabbits and the birds feasting under the tree!

I packed a ball of snow round and hard, slipped forward upon my knees and hurled it. Spat! it struck the end of a stick within an inch of the ugly head, nearly filling the crevice with snow. Instantly the head appeared at another crack, and another ball struck viciously beside it. Now it was back where it first appeared, nor did it flinch for the next ball, or the next. The third went true, striking with a chug and packing the crack. But the black, hating eyes were still watching me a foot lower down.

It is not all peace and good-will in the Christmas woods. But happily the weasels are few. More friendly and timid eyes were watching me than bold and murderous. It was foolish to want to kill—even the weasel, for one's woods are what one makes them. And so I let the man with the gun, who just then chanced along, think that I had turned boy again, and was snowballing the woodpile just for the fun of trying to hit the end of the biggest stick.

I was glad he had come. The sight of him took all hatred out of me. As he strode off with his stained bag I felt kindlier toward the weasel—there were worse in the woods than he. He must kill to live, and if he gloated over the kill, why, what fault of his? But the other, the one with the blood-stained game-bag, he killed for the love of killing. I was glad he had gone.

The crows were winging over toward their great

roost[33] in the pines when I turned toward the town. They, too, had had good picking along the creek flats and the ditches of the meadows. Their powerful wing-beats and constant play up in the air told of full crops and no fear for the night, already softly gray across the silent fields.

The air was crisper; the snow began to crackle underfoot; the twigs creaked and rattled as I brushed along; a brown beech leaf wavered down and skated with a thin scratch over the crust; and pure as the snow-wrapped crystal world, and sweet as the soft gray twilight, came the call of a quail.

These were not the voices, colors, odors, and forms of summer. The very face of things had changed; all had been reduced, made plain, simple, single, pure! There was less for the senses, but how much keener now their joy! The wide landscape, the frosty air, the tinkle of tiny icicles, and, out of the quiet of the falling twilight, the voice of the quail!

There is no day but is beautiful in the woods; and none more beautiful than one like this Christmas Day— warm, and still, and wrapped to the round red berries of the holly in the magic of the snow.

---

[33] *The crows were winging over toward their great roost:* Don't fail this winter to spend, if not Christmas Day, then one of your Christmas vacation days, in the woods, from morning until the crows go over to their roost. You will never forget that day.

CHAPTER VI

CHICKADEE

I WAS crunching along through the January dusk toward home. The cold was bitter. A half-starved partridge had just risen from the road and fluttered off among the naked bushes—a bit of life vanishing into the winter night of the woods. I knew the very hemlock in which he would roost; but what were the thick, snow-bent boughs of his hemlock, and what were all his winter feathers in such a night as this?—this night of cutting winds and frozen snow!

The road dipped from the woods down into a wide, open meadow, where the winds were free. The cold was driving, numbing here, with a power for death that the thermometer could not mark. I backed against the gale and sidewise hastened forward toward the double line of elms that arched the road in front of the house. Already I could hear them creak and rattle like things of glass. It was not the sound of life. Nothing was alive; for what could live in this long darkness and fearful cold?

The question was hardly thought, when an answer was whirled past me into the nearest of the naked elms. A chickadee! He caught for an instant on a dead stub of a limb that stuck out over the road, scrambled along to its broken tip, and whisked into a hole that ran straight

down the centre of the old stub, down, for I don't know how far.

I stopped. The limb lay out upon the wind, with only an eddy of the gale sucking at the little round hole in the broken end, while somewhere far down in its hollow heart, huddling himself into a downy, dozy ball for the night, had crept the chickadee. I knew by the very way he struck the limb and by the way he turned in at the hole that he had been there before. He knew whither, across the sweeping meadows, he was being blown. He had even helped the winds as they whirled him, for, having tarried along the roads until late, he was in a great hurry to get home. But he was safe for the night now, in the very bed, it may be, where he was hatched last summer, and where at this moment, who knows, were crowded half a dozen other chickadees, the rest of that last summer's brood, unharmed still, and still sharing the old home hollow, where they were as snug and warm this fierce, wild night as ever they were in the soft May days when they nestled here together.

The cold drove me on; but the sight of the chickadee had warmed me, and all my shivering world of night and death. And so he ever does. For the winter has yet to be that drives him seeking shelter to the sunny south. I never knew it colder than in January and February of 1904. During both of those months I drove morning and evening through a long mile of empty, snow-buried woods. For days at a time I would not see even a crow, but morning and evening at a certain dip in the road two chickadees would fly from bush to bush across the hollow and cheer me on my way.

They came out to the road, really to pick up whatever scanty crumbs of food were to be found in my wake. They came also to hear me, and to see me go past—to escape for a moment, I think, from the silence, the desertion, and the death of the woods. They helped me to escape, too.

Four other chickadees, all winter long, ate with us at the house, sharing, so far as the double windows would allow, the cheer of our dining-room. We served them their meals on the lilac bush outside the window, tying their suet on so that they could see us and we could see them during meal-time. Perhaps it was mere suet, and nothing else at all, that they got; but constantly, when our "pie was opened, the birds began to sing"—a dainty dish indeed, a dish of live, happy chickadees that fed our souls.

There are states in the far Northwest where the porcupine is protected by law, as a last food resource for men who are lost and starving in the forests. Porcupine is so slow that a dying man can catch him and make a meal on him. Perhaps the porcupine was not designed by nature for any such purpose, and would not approve of it at all. Perhaps Chickadee was not left behind by Summer to feed my lost and starving hope through the cheerless months of winter. But that is the use I make of him. He is Summer's pledge to me. He tells me that this winter world is a living world and not a dreary world of death. The woods are hollow, the winds are chill, the earth is cold and stiff, but there flits Chickadee, and—I cannot lose faith, nor feel that this procession of bleak white days is all a funeral! If Chickadee can live, then so can I.

He is the only bird in my out-of-doors that I can find without fail three hundred and sixty-five days in the year. From December to the end of March he comes daily to my lilac bush for suet; from April to early July he is busy with domestic cares in the gray birches down the hillside; from August to December he and his family come hunting quietly and sociably as a little flock among the trees and bushes of the farm; and from then on he is back again for his winter meals at "The Lilac."[34]

Is it any wonder that he was the first bird I ever felt personally acquainted with? That early acquaintance, however, was not brought about by his great abundance, nor by his very bad, bold manners, as might be with the English sparrow. I got acquainted with him first, because he wanted to get acquainted with me, he is such

---

[34] *"The Lilac"*: My lilac bush with its suet has become a kind of hotel, or inn, or boarding-house, for the chickadees.

a cheerful, confiding, sociable little bird! He drops down and peeps under your hat-brim to see what manner of boy you are, and if you are really fit to be abroad in this beautiful world, so altogether good both summer and winter—for chickadees.

He is not quite so sociable in summer as in winter, but if you were no bigger than a chickadee (two and one half inches without your tail!) and had eight babies nearly as big as yourself to hunt grubs for, besides a wife to pet and feed, do you think you could be very sociable? In the winter, however, he is always at liberty to stop and talk to you, a sweet little way he has that makes him the easiest bird in the world to get acquainted with.

Last winter while I was tying up a piece of suet that had fallen into the snow, a hungry and impatient chickadee lighted on the brim of my felt hat. The brim bent under him, and he came fluttering down against my nose, which I thought for an instant he was going to take for suet! He didn't snip it off, however, as a certain blackbird did a certain maiden's nose, but lighted instead on my shoulder. Then, seeing the lump of suet in my hand, he flew up and perched upon my fingers and held on, picking at the suet all the time I was tying it fast in the bush.

He is a friendly little soul, who loves your neighborhood, as, indeed, most birds do; who has no fear of you, because he cannot think that you could fear him and so would want to hurt him.

Nature made him an insect-eater; but he has a mission to perform besides eating pestiferous insects, and their eggs and grubs. This destruction of insects he does that the balance of things may be maintained out of doors, lest the insects destroy us. He has quite another work to do, which is not a matter of grubs, and which in no wise is a matter of fine feathers or sweet voice, but simply a matter of sweet nature, vigor, and concentrated cheerfulness.

Chickadee is a sermon. I hear him on a joyous May morning calling *Chick-a-dee! dee! Chick-a-dee! dee!*— brisk, bright, and cheery; or, soft and gentle as a caress, he whistles, *Phœ-ee-bee! Phœ-ee-bee!*[35] I meet him again on the edge of a bleak winter night. He is hungry and cold, and he calls, as I hasten along, *Chick-a-dee! dee! Chick-a-dee! dee!* brisk, bright, and cheery; or, following after me, he talks to me with words as soft and gentle as a caress.

Will you lend me your wings, Chickadee, your invisible wings on which you ride the winds of life so evenly?

The abundant summer, the lean and wolfish winter, find Chickadee cheerful and gentle. He is busier at some seasons than at others, with fewer chances for friendship. He almost disappears in the early summer. But this is because of family cares; and because the bigger, louder birds have come back, and the big leaves have come out and hidden him. A little searching, and

---

[35]*Phœ-ee-bee!* more often the spring call than the winter call of Chickadee. It is to be distinguished from the "phœ′be" call of the phœbe, the flycatcher, by its greater softness and purity, and by its very distinct *middle syllable*, as if Chickadee said "Phœ′—ee—bee." Phœbe's note is two-syllabled.

you will discover him, in one of your old decayed fence-posts, maybe, or else deep in the swamp, foraging for a family of from six to eight, that fairly bulge and boil over from the door of their home.

Here about Mullein Hill, this is sure to be a gray-birch home. Other trees will do—on a pinch. I have found Chickadee nesting in live white oaks, maples, upturned roots, and tumbling fence-posts. These were shifts, only, mere houses, not real homes. The only good homelike trees are old gray birches, dead these many years and gone to punk—mere shells of tough circular bark walls. Halfway down the hill is a small grove of these birches that we call the Seminary (because, as a poet friend says, "they look like seminary girls in white frocks"). Here the chickadees love to build.

Why has Chickadee this very decided preference? Is it a case of protective coloration[36]—the little gray and black bird choosing to nest in this little gray and black tree because bird and tree so exactly match one another in size and color? Or is there a strain of poetry in Chickadee's soul, something fine, that leads him into this exquisite harmony—into this little gray house for his little gray self?

Explain it as you may, it is a fact that the little bird shows this marked preference, makes this deliberate choice; and in the choice is protection and poetry,

---

[36]*protective coloration:* a favorite term with Darwin and many later naturalists to describe the wonderful harmony in the colors of animals, insects, etc., and their natural surroundings, the animal's color blending so perfectly into the color of its surroundings as to be a protection to the creature.

too. Doubtless he follows the guidance of a sure and watchful instinct. But who shall deny to him a share of the higher, finer things of the imagination?

His life is like his home—gentle and sweet and idyllic. There is no happier spot in the summer woods than that about the birch of the chickadees; and none whose happiness you will be so little liable to disturb.

Before the woods were in leaf last spring I found a pair of chickadees building in a birch along the edge of the swamp. They had just begun, having dug out only an inch of the cavity. It was very interesting to discover them doing the excavating themselves, for usually they refit some abandoned chamber or adapt to their needs some ready-made hole.

The birch was a long, limbless cylinder of bark, broken off about fourteen feet up, and utterly rotten, the mere skin of a tree stuffed with dust. I could push my finger into it at any point. It was so weak that every time the birds lighted upon the top the whole stub wobbled and reeled. Surely they were building their house upon the sand! Any creature without wings would have known that. The birds, however, because they have wings, seem to have lost the sense of such insecurity, often placing their nests as if they expected the nests themselves to take wings and fly to safety when the rains descend and the winds come.

This shaking stub of the chickadees was standing directly beneath a great overshadowing pine, where, if no partridge bumped into it, if two squirrels did not scamper up it together, if the crows nesting overhead in the pine did not discover it, if no strong wind bore down upon it from the meadow side, it might totter out the nesting-season. But it didn't. The birds were leaving too much to luck. I knew it, and perhaps I should have pushed their card house[37] down, then and there, and saved the greater ruin later. Perhaps so, but who was I to interfere in their labor?

Both birds were at the work when I discovered them, and so busily at it that my coming up did not delay them for a single billful. It was not hard digging, but it was very slow, for Chickadee is neither carpenter nor mason. He has difficulty killing a hard-backed beetle. So, whenever you find him occupying a clean-walled cavity, with a neat, freshly chipped doorway, you may be sure that some woodpecker built the house, and not this short-billed, soft-tailed little tit. Chickadee lacks both the bill chisel and the tail brace. Perhaps the explanation

---

[37]*card house:* as if made of cards, easily pushed, even blown down.

of his fondness for birch trees lies here—because the birch trees die young and soon decay!

The birds were going down through the broken-off top, and not by a hole through the leathery rind of the sides, for the bark was too tough for their beaks. They would drop into the top of the stub, pick up a wad of decayed wood and fly off to a dead limb of the pine. Here, with a jerk and a snap of their bills, they would scatter the punk in a shower so thin and far that I could neither hear it fall nor find a trace of it upon the dead leaves of the ground. This nest would never be betrayed by the workmen's chips,[38] as are the woodpeckers' nest-holes.

Between the pair there averaged three beakfuls of excavating every two minutes, one of the birds regularly shoveling twice to the other's once. They looked so exactly alike that I could not tell which bird was pushing the enterprise; but I had my suspicions. It was Mrs. Chickadee!

Mr. Chickadee was doing only part of his duty, and only half-heartedly at that! Hers was the real interest, the real anxiety. To be a Mr. Chickadee and show off! That's the thing!

I sat a long time watching the work. It went on in perfect silence, not a chirp, not the sound of a fluttering wing. The swamp along whose margin the birds were building had not a joyous atmosphere. Damp, dim-shadowed, and secret, it seemed to have laid its spell

---

[38]*the workman's chips:* Look on the ground under a newly excavated woodpecker's hole, and you will find his "chips."

upon the birds. Their very color of gray and black was as if mixed out of the dusky colors of the swamp; their noiseless coming and going was like the slipping to and fro of small shadows. They were a part of the swamp—of its life, of its color, of its silence. They were children of the swamp, sharing its very spirit, and that sharing was their defense, the best protection that they could have had.

It didn't save their nest, however. They felt and obeyed the spirit of the Swamp in their own conduct, but the Swamp did not tell them where to build. Birds and animals have wonderful instinct, or family wisdom, but not much personal, individual wisdom.

It was about three weeks later when I stopped again under the pine and found the birch stub in pieces upon the ground. Some strong wind had come, or some robber had been after the eggs, and had brought the whole house tumbling down.

But this is not the fate of all such birch-bark houses. Now and again they escape; yet when they do it is always a matter for wonder.

I was following an old disused wood-road once when I frightened a robin from her nest. Her mate joined her, and together they raised a great hubbub. Immediately a chewink, a pair of vireos, and two black and white warblers joined the robins in their din. Then a chickadee appeared. He had a worm in his beak. His anxiety seemed so real that I began to watch him, when, looking down among the stones for a place to step, what should I see but his mate emerging from the end of a tiny birch stump at my very feet! She had heard the racket and had come out to see what it was all about. At sight of her, Mr. Chickadee hastened with his worm, brushing my face, almost, as he darted to her side. She took the worm sweetly, for she knew he had intended it for her. But how do I know it was intended for her, and not for the young? There were no young in the nest; only eggs. Even after the young came (there were eight of them!), when life, from daylight to dark, was one ceaseless, hurried hunt for worms, I saw him over and over again fly to Mrs. Chickadee's side caressingly and tempt her to eat.

The house of this pair did not fall. How could it when it stood precisely two and a half feet from the ground? But that it wasn't looted is due to the amazing boldness of its situation. It stood alone, close to the road, so close that the hub of a low wheel in passing might have knocked it down. Perhaps a hundred persons had brushed it in going by. How many dogs and cats had overlooked it no one can say; nor how many skunks and snakes and squirrels. The accident that discovered it to me had happened apparently to no one else, so here it stood still safe, but only by the grace of Luck!

Cutting a tiny window[39] in the bark just above the eggs, I looked in upon the little children every day. I watched them hatch, grow, and fill the cavity and hang over at the top. I was there the day they forced my window open; I was there the day when there was

[39] *a tiny window:* The tough birch-bark would bend readily. I would shut the window in leaving by means of a long, sharp thorn.

no more room at the top, and when, at the call of their parents, one child after another of this large, sweet bird family found his wings and flew away through the friendly woods.

CHAPTER VII

A CHAPTER OF THINGS TO DO THIS WINTER

I

YOU should go skating—crawling, I ought to say—over a pond of glare ice this winter. Take the pond you are most familiar with. Go early on a bright day, before any skater arrives, and lying flat upon the clear, "black" ice, study the bottom of the pond and the fish that swim below you. They have boats with glass bottoms along the California coast, through which to watch the marvelous bottoms off shore. But an Eastern pond covered with glare ice is as good, for such ice is a plate-glass window into a wonder world.

II

Fight your way one of these winter days to the crest of some high hill and stand up against a northwest gale. Feel the sweep of the winds from across the plain beneath you; hear them speaking close in your ear, as they fly past; catch them and breathe them, until they

76

run red in your leaping veins. Master them, and make them, mighty as they are, your own. And something large and free, strong and sound will pass into you; and you will love the great world more, and you will feel how fit a place, for the strong of heart, is this earth to live on.

III

Keep a careful list of the winter birds you see; and visit every variety of wood, meadow, and upland in your neighborhood—not neglecting the parks and city trees—for a sight of the rarer winter visitors, such as the snowy owl, the snow buntings, and the crossbills.

IV

If you know little about the birds, then this is the time to begin your study. When they are so few and scarce? Yes, just because they are few and scarce. On a June morning (unless you are at home in the woods) you will be confused by the medley of songs you hear, and the shapes flitting everywhere about you; and you may be tempted to give up your study for the very multitude. Get a pair of good field or opera glasses and a good bird book, such as Hoffmann's *Guide to the Birds*, and go into the fields and woods—leaving the book at home.

The first bird you see follow up until you can remember (1) his size, color—whether he has a white bar on wings, or small spots or large clear spots on breast; (2) his chirp, or call; (3) something peculiar about his flight—a flirt of the tail, a habit of flying down to the ground in getting away. Then come back to your book and identify him from memory. If you cannot, then go out again and again; and it will not be long before either this first one, or others, will be accurately made out—the beginning of an acquaintance that you can extend in the summer, but which will be plenty large enough for your "coming-out" winter into bird society. For here is a list of the birds you may be able to find during the winter:—

Screech owl, crow, robin, flicker, jay, goldfinch, tree sparrow, English sparrow, song sparrow, junco, golden-crowned kinglet, nuthatch, brown creeper, downy woodpecker, quail, partridge.

V

See to it that no bird in your neighborhood starves for lack of food that you can supply. Tie a piece of suet to a tree or bush near the house (by the window if you can) for the chickadees and blue jays; keep a place on the lawn cleared of snow and well supplied with crumbs and small seeds for the juncos and the sparrows; hang a netted bag of cracked nuts out some where for the nuthatches; and provide corn and nuts for the squirrels.

VI

Go out on a cold December day, or a January day, and see how many "signs" of spring—"Minor Prophets," as Mr. Torrey calls them—you can bring home. They will be mostly buds of various sorts. Then, on a warm, soft day, go again to see what you can bring home—flitting, creeping, crawling things that the warm sun has brought from their winter hiding.

VII

Make a map of your sky, showing the positions of the planets, the constellations, and the most brilliant stars, the points in the horizon for the rising and setting of the sun, say, in January, noting the changes in places of things since your last map drawn in October. Any school child can do it, and, in doing it, learn the few large facts about the sky that most people are pitifully ignorant of.

VIII

Go out after a fresh light snow and take up the trail of a fox or a rabbit or a partridge, as you might take up a problem in arithmetic, or as a detective might take up a clew, and "solve" it—where the creature came from, w h e r e g o i n g , what for, in a hurry or not, pursued or pursuing, etc. It will give you one of the best of lessons in observation, in following a clew, and in learning to take a hint.

IX

Go out to study the face of the ground—the ridges, hollows, level places, the ledges, meadows, sandbanks, the course of the streams, the location of the springs— the general shape and contour, the pitch and slant and make-up of the region over which you tramp in the summer. Now, when the leaves are off and things swept bare, you can get a general idea of the lay of the land that will greatly aid you in your more detailed study of

plants and birds, of individual things, in the summer.
It is like an outline map in your geography.

X

Winter is the time to do much good reading. A
tramp over real fields is to be preferred to a tramp in
a book. But a good book is pretty nearly as good as
anything under the stars. You need both fields and
books. And during these cold days—impossible days,
some of them, for work afield—you will read, read. Oh,
the good things to read[40] that have been written about
the out-of-doors!

[40]*the good things to read:* To name only a few of them,
we might mention John Burroughs's *Winter Sunshine* and
Squirrels and Other Fur-Bearers, Bradford Torrey's *Footing It
in Franconia*, Frank Bolles's *At the North of Bearcamp Water*,
William Hamilton Gibson's *Eye Spy*, William L. Finley's
American Birds, and Edward Breck's *Wilderness Pets*.

CHAPTER VIII

THE MISSING TOOTH

THE snow had melted from the river meadows, leaving them flattened, faded, and stained with mud—a dull, dreary waste in the gray February. I had stopped beside a tiny bundle of bones that lay in the matted grass a dozen feet from a ditch. Here, still showing, was the narrow path along which the bones had dragged themselves; there the hole by which they had left the burrow in the bank of the ditch. They had crawled out in this old runway, then turned off a little into the heavy autumn grass and laid them down. The rains had come and the winter snows. The spring was breaking now and the small bundle, gently loosened and uncovered, was whitening on the wide, bare meadow.

Shall I stop beside this small bundle of whitening bones or shall I turn my head away and pass on? Shall I allow you to stop with me in our winter ramble and let you see the tragedy here in the flattened meadow grass, or shall I hide from your eyes the dark, the bitter, the tragic in the lives of the wild things out of doors?

I think it is best to hide nothing from you. Real love for nature is largely sympathy with nature; and there can be no sympathy without intimate and full understanding of the struggle and suffering in the lives out of doors. There is a dark story in this little bundle of bones. Do you wish to hear it? There is a fierce, cruel threat in the growl of the winter wind. Do you wish to hear that? There is menace and death in the shrill scream of the hawk. Do you wish to hear that? Or do you wish to hear only the song of the robin? only the whisper of the summer breeze? only the story of the life and love and joy of things?

No, there are two sides to life—two sides to your life, the bright and dark sides; two sides to the lives of all men, and to the lives of all things. Summer is the bright side of Nature's life; winter is the dark side. Summer and winter are both needed to round out the life of the year; so tears and laughter seem to be needed in our lives; joy and sorrow, peace and suffering, rest and hardship—these, or something like them, seem to be needed in the lesser lives of birds and beasts to round out their experience and make them keen and strong.

Happily, the pain and suffering in nature are largely hidden from us. Wild things when stricken "turn their faces to the wall," retreat, slink silently away out of sight to be alone. They do not wish us to know. But we do know, and we need to know, if we would enter into their lives as a sharer in them; and if we would enter into and understand the larger, wider, deeper life of which they, and we, and all things, are a part.

You must pause with me above this little bundle of bones until I tell you their story.

I had recognized the bones at once as the skeleton of a muskrat. But it was something peculiar in the way they lay that had caused me to pause. They seemed outstretched, as if composed by gentle hands, the hands of sleep. They had not been flung down. The delicate ribs had fallen in, but not a bone was broken nor displaced, not one showed the splinter of shot, or the crack that might have been made by a steel trap. No violence had been done them. They had been touched by nothing rougher than the snow. Out into the hidden runway they had crept. Death had passed by them here; but no one else in all the winter months.

The creature had died—a "natural" death. It had starved, while a hundred acres of plenty lay round about. Picking up the skull, I found the jaws locked together as if they were a single solid bone. One of the two incisor teeth[41] of the upper jaw was missing, and apparently had never developed. The opposite tooth on the lower jaw, thus unopposed and so unworn, had grown beyond its normal height up into the empty socket above, then on, turning outward and piercing the cheek-bone in front of the eye, whence, curving like a boar's tusk, it had slowly closed the jaws and locked them, rigid, set, as fixed as jaws of stone.

---

[41] *incisor teeth:* the four long front teeth of the rodents,—rats, mice, beavers, etc. These incisor teeth are heavily enameled with a sharp cutting edge and keep growing continuously.

At first the animal had been able to gnaw; but as the tooth curved through the bones of the face and gradually tightened the jaws, the creature got less and less to eat, until, one day, creeping out of the burrow for food, the poor thing was unable to get back.

We seldom come upon the like of this. It is commoner than we think; but, as I have said, it is usually hidden away and quickly over. How often do we see a wild thing sick—a bird or animal suffering from an accident, or dying, like this muskrat, because of some physical defect? The struggle between animals—the falling of the weak as prey to the strong—is ever before us; but this single-handed fight between the creature and Nature is a far rarer, silenter tragedy. Nature is too swift to allow us time for sympathy.

At best there is only a fighting chance in the meadow. Only strength and craft may win; only those who have all of their teeth. The muskrat with a single missing tooth never enters the real race of life at all. He slinks from some abandoned burrow, and, if the owl and mink are not watching, he dies alone in the grass, and we rarely know.

I shall never forget the impression made upon me by those quiet bones. It was like that made by my first visit to a great city hospital—out of the busy, cheerful street into a surgical ward, where the sick and injured lay in long white lines. We tramp the woods and meadows and never step from the sweet air and the pure sunlight of health into a hospital. But that is not because no sick, ill-formed, or injured are there.

The proportion is smaller than among us humans, and for very good reasons, yet there is much real suffering, and to come upon it, as we will, now and then, must certainly quicken our understanding and deepen our sympathy with the life out of doors.

No sensible person could for a moment believe the animals capable of suffering as a human being can suffer; nor that there is any such call for our sympathy from them as from our human neighbors. But an unselfish sharing of the life of the fields demands that we take part in all of it.

Nature wears a brave face. Her smile is ever in the open, her laughter quick and contagious. This brave front is no mask. It is real. Sunlight, song, color, form, and fragrance are real. And so is our love and joy in Nature real. Real, also, should be our sympathy and sorrow with Nature.

Here, for instance, are my crows: do I share fully in the life of Nature so long as I think of the crow only with admiration for his cunning or with wrath at his destruction of my melons and corn?

A crow has his solemn moments. He knows fear, pain, hunger, accident, and disease; he knows something very like affection and love. For all that, he is a mere crow. But a mere crow is no mean thing. He is my brother, and a real love will give me part in all his existence. I will forage and fight with him; I will parley and play; and when the keen north winds find him in the frozen pines, I will suffer with him, too.

Here again are my meadow voles.[42] I know that my hay crop is shorter every year for them,—a very little shorter. And I can look with satisfaction at a cat carrying a big bob-tailed vole out of my "mowing," for the voles, along with other mice, are injurious to man.

But one day I came upon two of my voles struggling for life in the water, exhausted and well-nigh dead. I helped them out, as I should have helped out any other creature, and having saved them, why, what could I do but let them go—even into my own meadow? This has happened several times.

When the drought dries the meadow, the voles come to the deep, plank-walled spring at the upper end, to drink. The water usually trickles over the curb, but in a long dry spell it shrinks to a foot or more below the edge, and the voles, once within for their drink, cannot get out. Time and again I had fished them up, until I thought to leave a board slanting down to the water, so that they could climb back to the top.

It is wholesome to be the good Samaritan to a meadow mouse, to pour out, even waste, a little of the oil and wine of sympathy on the humblest of our needy neighbors.

[42]*voles:* meadow mice.

Here are the chimney swallows,[43] too. One can look with complacency, with gratitude, indeed, upon the swallows of other chimneys, as they hawk in the sky; yet, when the little creatures, so useful, but so uncombed and unfumigated, set up their establishments in your chimney, to the jeopardy of the whole house, then you need an experience like mine.

I had had a like experience years before, when the house did not belong to me. This time, however, the house was mine, and if it became infested with vermin[44] because of the swallows, I could not move away; so I felt like burning them in the chimney, bag and baggage. There were four nests, as nearly as I could make out, and, from the frequent squeakings, I knew they were all filled with young. Then one day, when the young were nearly ready to fly, there came a rain that ran wet far down the sooty chimney, loosened the mortar of the nests, and sent them crashing into the fireplace.

Some of the young birds were killed outright; the others were at my mercy, flung upon me,—helpless, wailing infants! Of course I made it comfortable for them on the back-log, and let their mothers flutter down unhindered to feed them. Had I understood the trick, I would have hawked for them and helped feed them myself!

They made a great thunder in the chimney; they rattled down into the living-room a little soot; but

---

[43] *chimney swallows:* more properly swifts; as these birds do not belong to the swallow family at all.

[44] *vermin:* The swifts are generally infested with vermin.

nothing further came of it. We were not quarantined. On the contrary, we had our reward, according to promise; for it was an extremely interesting event to us all. It dispelled some silly qualms, it gave us intimate part in a strange small life, so foreign, yet so closely linked to our own; and it made us pause with wonder that even our empty, sooty chimney could be made use of by Nature to our great benefit.

I wonder if the nests of the chimney swallows came tumbling down when the birds used to build in caves and hollow trees? It is a most extraordinary change, this change from the trees to the chimneys, and it does not seem to have been accompanied by an increase of architectural wisdom necessary to meet all the conditions of the new hollow. The mortar or glue, which, I imagine, held firmly in the empty trees, will not mix with the chimney soot, so that the nest, especially when crowded with young, is easily loosened by the rain, and sometimes even broken away by the slight wing stroke of a descending swallow, or by the added weight of a parent bird as it settles with food.

We little realize how frequent fear is among the birds and animals, and how often it proves fatal. A situation that would have caused no trouble ordinarily, becomes through sudden fright a tangle or a trap. I have known many a quail to bolt into a fast express train and fall dead. Last winter I left the large door of the barn open, so that my flock of juncos could feed inside upon the floor. They found their way into the hayloft and went up and down freely. On two or three occasions I happened in so suddenly that they were thoroughly frightened and flew madly into the cupola to escape through the windows. They beat against the glass until utterly dazed, and would have perished there, had I not climbed up later and brought them down. So thousands of the migrating birds perish yearly by flying wildly against the dazzling lanterns of the lighthouses, and thousands more either lose their course in the thick darkness of the stormy nights, or else are blown out of it, and drift far away to sea.

Hasty, careless, miscalculated movements are not as frequent among the careful wild folk as among us, perhaps; but there is abundant evidence of their occasional occurrence and of their sometimes fatal results.

Several instances are recorded of birds that have been tangled in the threads of their nests; and one instance of a bluebird that was caught in the flying meshes of an oriole's nest into which it had been spying.

I once found the mummied body of a chippy twisting and swinging in the leafless branches of a peach tree. The little creature was suspended in a web of horsehair about two inches below a nest. It looked as if she had brought a snarled bunch of the hair and left it loose in the twigs. Later on, a careless step and her foot was fast, when every frantic effort for freedom only tangled her the worse. In the nest above were four other tiny mummies—a double tragedy that might with care have been averted.

A similar fate befell a song sparrow that I discovered hanging dead upon a barbed-wire fence. By some chance it had slipped a foot through an open place between the two twisted strands, and then, fluttering along, had wedged the leg and broken it in the struggle to escape.

We have all held our breath at the hazardous traveling of the squirrels in the treetops. What other animals take such risks?—leaping at dizzy heights from bending limbs to catch the tips of limbs still smaller, saving themselves again and again by the merest chance.

But luck sometimes fails. My brother, a careful watcher in the woods, on one occasion when he was hunting, saw a gray squirrel miss its footing in a tree and fall, breaking its neck upon a log beneath.

I have frequently known squirrels to fall short distances, and once I saw a red squirrel come to grief like this gray squirrel. He was scurrying through the tops of some lofty pitch pines, a little hurried and flustered at sight of me, and, nearing the end of a high branch, was in the act of springing, when the dead tip cracked under him and he came tumbling headlong.

The height must have been forty feet, so that before he reached the ground he had righted himself,—his tail out and legs spread,—but the fall was too great. He hit the earth heavily, and before I could reach him he lay dead upon the needles, with blood oozing from his eyes and nostrils.

Unhoused and often unsheltered, the wild things suffer as we hardly yet understand. No one can estimate how many of our wild creatures die in a year from severe cold, heavy storms, high winds and tides. I have known the nests of a whole colony of gulls and terns to be swept away in a great storm; while the tides, over and over, have flooded the inlet marshes and drowned out the nests in the grass—those of the clapper rails[45] by thousands.

I remember a late spring storm that came with the returning redstarts and, in my neighborhood, killed many of them. Toward evening of that day one of the little black-and-orange voyageurs fluttered against the window and we let him in, wet, chilled, and so exhausted that for a moment he lay on his back in my open palm. Soon after there was another soft tapping at the window,—and two little redstarts were sharing our cheer and drying their butterfly wings in our warmth. Both of these birds would have perished had we not harbored them for the night.

The birds and animals are not as weather-wise as we; they cannot foretell as far ahead nor provide as certainly against need, despite the popular notion to the contrary.

We point to the migrating birds, to the muskrat houses, to the hoards of the squirrels, and say, "How wise and far-sighted these Nature-taught children are!" True, they are, but only for conditions that are normal. Their wisdom does not cover the unusual. The

[45] *clapper rails:* or marsh-hens *(Rallus crepitans).*

gray squirrels did not provide for the unusually hard weather of last winter. Three of them from the woodlot came begging of me, and lived on my wisdom, not their own.

Consider the ravens, that neither sow nor reap, that have neither storehouse nor barn, yet they are fed—but not always. Indeed, there are few of our winter birds that go hungry so often as do the cousins of the ravens, the crows, and that die in so great numbers for lack of food and shelter.

After severe and protracted cold, with a snow-covered ground, a crow-roost looks like a battlefield, so thick lie the dead and wounded. Morning after morning the flock goes over to forage in the frozen fields, and night after night returns hungrier, weaker, and less able to resist the cold. Now, as the darkness falls, a bitter wind breaks loose and sweeps down upon the pines.

> "List'ning the doors an' winnocks rattle,
> I thought me on the ourie cattle,"—[46]

and how often I have thought me of the crows biding the night yonder in the moaning pines! So often, as a boy, and with so real an awe, have I watched them returning at night, that the crows will never cease flying through my wintry sky,—an endless line of wavering black figures, weary, retreating figures, beating over in the early dusk.

And to-night another wild storm sweeps across the winter fields. All the afternoon the crows have

[46] *"List'ning the doors an' winnocks rattle"*: lines from Burns's "A Winter Night."

93

been going over, and are still passing as the darkness settles at five o'clock. Now it is nearly eight, and the long night is but just begun. The storm is increasing. The wind shrieks about the house, whirling the fine snow in hissing eddies past the corners and driving it on into long, curling crests across the fields. I can hear the roar as the wind strikes the shoal of pines where the fields roll into the woods—a vast surf sound, but softer and higher, with a wail like the wail of some vast heart in pain.

I can see the tall trees rock and sway with their burden of dark forms. As close together as they can crowd on the bending limbs cling the crows, their breasts turned all to the storm. With crops empty and bodies weak, they rise and fall in the cutting, ice-filled wind for thirteen hours of night.

Is it a wonder that the life fires burn low? that sometimes the small flames flicker and go out?

CHAPTER IX

THE PECULIAR 'POSSUM

IF you are a New Englander, or a Northwesterner, then, probably, you have never pulled a 'possum out of his hollow stump or from under some old rail-pile, as I have done, many a time, down in southern New Jersey. And so, probably, you have never made the acquaintance of the most peculiar creature in our American woods.

Even roast 'possum is peculiar. Up to the time you taste roast 'possum you quite agree with Charles Lamb[47] that roast pig is peculiarly the most delicious delicacy "in the whole *modus edibilis*,"[48] in other words, bill of fare. But once you eat roast 'possum, you will go all over Lamb's tasty "Dissertation upon Roast Pig," marking out "pig" with your pencil and writing in "'possum," making the essay read thus:—

"There is no flavor comparable, I will contend, to that of the crisp, tawny, well-watched, not over-roasted, *'possum*, as it is called,—the very teeth are invited to their

[47] *Charles Lamb:* Look up his life in the Encyclopedia. Read for yourselves his essay on Roast Pig.

[48] *modus edibilis:* the Latin for "manner of eating."

95

share of the pleasure at this banquet in overcoming the coy, brittle resistance,—with the adhesive oleaginous—O call it not fat! but an indefinable sweetness growing up to it—the tender blossoming of fat—fat cropped in the bud—taken in the shoot—in the first innocence—" For no matter how old your roast 'possum, he is as tender as the tenderest roast pig. And that, of course, is peculiar.

But live 'possum is more peculiar than roast 'possum. It is peculiar, for instance, that almost all of the 'possum's relations,[49] except his immediate family, dwell apart in Australia,—in Australasia, for marsupials are found also in Tasmania, New Guinea, and the Moluccas—which islands the marsupials seem to have had given them for their own when the world was made. There, at least, most of them live and have lived for ages, except the 'possums. These latter, strangely enough, live in South and North America, and nowhere else. The peculiar, puzzling thing about them is: how they, and they only of the marsupials, got away from Australia across the sea to America. Did a family of them get set adrift on a log and float across? Or was there once, as geologists tell us, a long string of islands close together, stretching from the tip of South America, from the "Horn," off across the sea to Australia, over which the 'possums might once have made their way? But if they came by such a route, why did not the kangaroos come too? Ah, the kangaroo is not a 'possum. There is no other creature in the woods that would dare play "Follow the leader"

[49] *the 'possum's relations:* They are the marsupials, the pouched animals, like the kangaroo.

with the 'possum. No, I am half inclined to think the scientists right who say that the 'possum is the great-great-grandfather of all the marsupials, and that the migration might have been the other way about—from America, across the sea.

But what is the use of speculating? Here is the 'possum in our woods; that we know; and yonder in Australasia are his thirteen sets of cousins, and there they seem always to have been, for of these thirteen sets of cousins, four sets have so long since ceased to live that they are now among the fossils, slowly turning, every one of them, to stone!

A queer history he has, surely! But queerer than his history, is his body, and the way he grows from babyhood to twenty-pound 'possumhood.

For besides having a tail that can be used for a hand, and a paw with a thumb like the human thumb, the female 'possum has a pocket or pouch on her abdomen, just as the kangaroo has, in which she carries her young.

Now that is peculiar, so very peculiar when you study deeply into it, that the 'possum becomes to the scientist quite the most interesting mammal in North America.

Returning from a Christmas vacation one year, while a student in college, I brought back with me twenty-six live 'possums so that the professor of zoölogy could study the peculiar anatomy of the 'possum for several of its many meanings.

This pouch, for instance, and the peculiar bones of the 'possum, show that it is a very primitive mammal, one of the very oldest mammals, so close to the beginning of the mammalian line that there are only two other living "animals" (we can hardly call them mammals) older and more primitive—the porcupine ant-eater, and, oldest of all, the duck-bill, not "older" at all perhaps, but only more primitive.

For the duck-bill, though classed as a mammal, not only has the bill of the duck, but also lays eggs like the birds. The porcupine ant-eater likewise lays eggs, and so seems almost as much bird or reptile as mammal. And as the birds and reptiles lived upon the earth before the age of mammals, and are a lower and more primitive order of creatures, so the duck-bill, the porcupine ant-eater, and the 'possum, because in their anatomy they are like the birds and the reptiles in some respects, are perhaps the lowest and the oldest of all the mammals.

The 'possum, therefore, is one of the most primitive of mammals, and dates as far back as the reptilian age,[50] when only traces of mammalian life are to be found, the 'possum's fossil ancestors being among the notable of these early remains.

The mammals at that time, as I have just said, were only partly mammal, for they were partly bird or reptile, as the duck-bill and ant-eater still are. Now the 'possum does not lay eggs as these other two do, for its young are born, not hatched; yet so tiny and undeveloped are they when born, that they must be put into their mother's pouch and nursed, as eggs are put into a nest and brooded until they are hatched—really born a second time.

For here in their mother's pouch they are like chicks in the shell, and quite as helpless. It is five weeks before they can stick their heads out and take a look at the world.

No other mammalian baby is so much of a baby and yet comes so near to being no baby at all. It is less than an inch long when put into the pouch, and it weighs

[50]*reptilian age:* one of the great geological ages or eras, known to the geologists as the great mesozoic or "middle" epoch, when reptiles ruled the land and sea.

only four grains! Four grains? Think how small that is. For there are 7000 grains to a pound, which means that it would take 1750 baby 'possums to weigh as much as two cups of sugar!

"I should say he was peculiar!" I hear you exclaim; and you will agree with an ancient History of Carolina which I have, when it declares: "The Opossum is the wonder of all the land animals."

I wish you had been with me one spring day as I was stretching a "lay-out" line across Cubby Hollow. (A lay-out line is a long fish-line, strung with baited hooks, and reaching across the pond from shore to shore.) I was out in the middle of the pond, lying flat on a raft made of three cedar rails, when my dog began to bark at something in a brier-patch on shore.

Paddling in as fast as I could, I found the dog standing

before a large 'possum, which was backed up against a tree. I finally got Mrs. 'Possum by the tail and dropped her unhurt into my eel-pot—a fish-trap made out of an empty nail-keg—which I had left since fall among the bushes of the hillside. Then paddling again to the middle of the pond, I untangled and set my hooks on the lay-out line, and came back to shore for my 'possum.

I didn't quite fancy pushing my hand down through

the burlap cover over the end of the keg; so I turned it upside down to spill the 'possum out,—and out she spilled and nine little 'possums with her!

I had put in one and spilled out—ten! And this proves again that the 'possum is peculiar. Nine of these were babies that had been hidden from me and the dog in their mother's pouch.

Peculiar, too, was the history of one of these nine young 'possums (the one we named "Pinky"). For after Pinky's mother choked to death on a fish-bone, I gave all his brothers and sisters away, and devoted myself to training Pinky up in the way he should go. And strangely enough, when he was grown, unlike any other wild animal I had ever tamed, he would not depart from these domesticated ways, but insisted upon coming back home every time I took him away to the woods.

Of course he was only a few months old when I tried to turn him loose in the woods, and that may account for his returning and squeezing through the opening of the pump-box trough into the kitchen and going fast asleep on the cushion of the settee; as it may also account for his getting into a neighbor's yard by mistake on his way back one night and drowning in the well.

You have read of 'possum hunts;—and they are peculiar, too, as naturally they must needs be. For you hunt 'possums with rabbit hounds, and shoot them with a meal-sack—shoot them *into* a meal-sack would be more exact. And you hunt by moonlight if you really love 'possum.

We used to start out just as the moon, climbing over the woods, fell soft across the bare fields. The old dog would be some distance ahead, her nose to the ground, sometimes picking up a trail in the first cornfield, or again not until we reached the woods, or again leading us for miles along the creek meadows among the scattered persimmon trees, before striking a fresh scent.

Wherever the trail started it usually led away for the woods, for some hollow stump or tree, where the 'possum made his nest. Once in a while I have overtaken the fat fellow in an open field or atop a fence, or have even caught him in a hencoop; but usually, if hunting at night, it has been a long, and not always an easy, chase, for a 'possum, in spite of his fat and his fossil ancestors, is not stupid. Or else he is so slow-witted that there is no telling, by man or dog, which way he will go, or what he may do next.

A rabbit, or a deer, or a coon, when you are on their trail, will do certain things. You can count upon them with great certainty. But a 'possum never seems to do anything twice alike; he has no traveled paths, no regular tricks, no set habits. He knows the road home, but it is always a different road—a meandering, roundabout, zigzag, criss-cross, up-and-down (up-the-trees-and-down) road, we-won't-get-home-till-morning road, that takes in all the way stations, from the tops of tall persimmon trees to the bottoms of all the deep, dark holes that need looking into, along the route.

Peculiar!—So, at least, a dog with an orderly mind and well-regulated habits thinks, anyhow. For a 'possum trail will give a good rabbit dog the blues; he hasn't the patience for it. Only a slow rheumatic old hound will stick to a 'possum trail with the endurance necessary to carry it to its end—in a hollow log, or a hollow stump, or under a shock of corn or a rail-pile. Once the trail actually led me, after much trouble, into a hen-house and into a stove in the hen-house, where, upon the grate, I found three 'possums in their nest!

It is a peculiar sport, this 'possum-hunting; yet it is mildly exciting; and when you get your 'possum by the tail, he smiles at you[51]—grins, I ought to say—and has a fit. To go hunting for a creature that smiles at you in a dreadful manner when you capture him, that

---

[51]*smiles at you—grins:* Read the account of this habit in the opening chapter of the author's *Wild Life Near Home.*

flops down in a dead faint or has a fit when you take him up by the tail, that shows the spunk and fight of a boiled cabbage—to go hunting for such a beast must be exciting, as exciting as going to the store for a quart of beans.

But here are the winter woods at night, and the wide, moonlit fields, covered, it may be, with the glistening snow. The full, round moon rides high overhead, the pointed corn-shocks stand silent over the fields, the woods rise dark and shadowy beyond. Only the slow, musical cry of the hound echoes through the stirless air, which seems to sparkle like the snow, as if filled with gleaming frost-dust that only the moonlight can catch and set to glancing silvery-bright.

You don't care whether you catch a 'possum or not; you are abroad in a world so large and silent, so crystal-clear and shining, so crisp, so open, so a-creep with shadows, so deep and mysterious in its distances, so pure and beautiful and unblemished, that just to be abroad is wonder enough, and you are not sorry to come back under the brilliant midnight sky with the old dog at your heels and over your shoulder an empty bag.

But if your bag is heavy with fat 'possum then that, too, is good. You have peered into his black hole; you have reached in and pulled him out—nothing more. No roar of a gun has shattered your world of crystal; you have killed nothing, wounded nothing—no, not even the silence and the serenity of your soul. You and the clear, calm night are still one.

You have dropped a smiling 'possum into an easy, roomy bag. He feels warm against your back. The old dog follows proud and content at your heels. And you feel—as the wide, softly shining sky seems to feel.

And that, too, is peculiar.

CHAPTER X

A FEBRUARY FRESHET

ONE of the very interesting events in my out-of-door year is the February freshet. Perhaps you call it the February *thaw*. That is all it could be called this year; and, in fact, a *thaw* is all that it ever is for me, nowadays, living, as I do, high and dry here, on Mullein Hill, above a sputtering little trout brook that could not have a freshet if it tried.

But Maurice River could have a freshet without trying. Let the high south winds, the high tides, and the warm spring rains come on together, let them drive in hard for a day and a night, as I have known them to do, and the deep, dark river goes mad! The tossing tide sweeps over the wharves, swirls about the piles of the great bridge, leaps foaming into the air, and up and down its long high banks beats with all its wild might to break through into the fertile meadows below.

There are wider rivers, and other, more exciting things, than spring freshets; but there were not when I was a boy. Why, Maurice River was so wide that there was but a single boy in the town, as I remember, who could stand at one end of the drawbridge and skim an oyster-shell over to the opposite end! The best that I could do was to throw my voice across and hear it echo from the long, hollow barn on the other bank. It would seem to me to strike the barn in the middle, leap from end to end like a creature caged, and then bound back to me faint and frightened from across the dark tide.

I feared the river. Oh, but I loved it, too. Its tides were always rising or falling—going down to the Delaware Bay and on to the sea. And in from the bay, or out to the bay, with white sails set, the big boats were always moving. And when they had gone, out over the wide water the gulls or the fish hawks would sail, or a great blue heron, with wings like the fans of an old Dutch mill, would beat ponderously across.

I loved the river. I loved the sound of the calking-maul and the adze in the shipyard, and the smell of the chips and tarred oakum; the chatter of the wrens among the reeds and calamus; the pink of the mallow and wild roses along the high mud banks; the fishy ditches with their deep sluiceways through the bank into the river;

and the vast, vast tide-marshes that, to this day, seem to me to stretch away to the very edge of the world.

What a world for a boy to drive cows into every morning, and drive them home from every night, as I used to help do! or to trap muskrats in during the winter; to go fishing in during the summer; to go splashing up and down in when the great February freshet came on!

For of all the events of the year, none had such fascination for me as the high winds and warm downpour that flooded the wharves, that drove the men of the village out to guard the river-banks, and that drowned out of their burrows and winter hiding-places all the wild things that lived within reach of the spreading tide.

The water would pour over the meadows and run far back into the swamps and farm lands, setting everything afloat that could float—rails, logs, branches; upon which, as chance offered, some struggling creature would crawl, and drift away to safety.

But not always to safety; for over the meadows the crows and fish hawks, gulls, herons, bitterns, and at night the owls, were constantly beating to pounce upon the helpless voyagers, even taking the muskrats, an easy prey, through their weakness from exposure and long swimming in the water.

There would be only two shores to this wild meadow-sea—the river-bank, a mere line of earth drawn through the water, and the distant shore of the upland. If the wind blew from the upland toward the bank, then the drift would all set that way, and before long a multitude of shipwrecked creatures would be tossed upon this narrow breakwater, that stood, a bare three feet of clay, against the wilder river-sea beyond.

To walk up and down the bank then was like entering a natural history museum where all the specimens were alive; or like going to a small menagerie. Sparrows, finches, robins, mice, moles, voles, shrews, snakes, turtles, squirrels, muskrats, with even a mink and an opossum now and then, would scurry from beneath your feet or dive back into the water as you passed along.

And by what strange craft they sometimes came! I once saw two muskrats and a gray squirrel floating along on the top of one of the muskrats' houses. And again a little bob-tailed meadow mouse came rocking

along in a drifting catbird's nest which the waves had washed from its anchorage in the rose-bushes. And out on the top of some tall stake, or up among the limbs of a tree you would see little huddled bunches of fur, a muskrat perhaps that had never climbed before in his life, waiting, like a sailor lashed to the rigging, to be taken off.

But it was not the multitude of wild things—birds, beasts, insects—that fascinated me most, that led me out along the slippery, dangerous bank through the swirling storm; it was rather the fear and confusion of the animals, the wild giant-spirit raging over the face of the earth and sky, daunting and terrifying them, that drew me.

Many of the small creatures had been wakened by the flood out of their deep winter sleep, and, dazed and numbed and frightened, they seemed to know nothing, to care for nothing but the touch of the solid earth to their feet.

All of their natural desires and instincts, their hatreds, hungers, terrors, were sunk beneath the waters. They had lost their wits, like human creatures in a panic, and, struggling, fighting for a foothold, they did not notice me unless I made at them, and then only took to the water a moment to escape the instant peril.

The sight was strange, as if this were another planet and not our orderly, peaceful world at all. Nor, indeed, was it; for fear cowered everywhere, in all the things that were of the earth, as over the earth and everything upon it raged the fury of river and sky.

The frail mud bank trembled under the beating of the waves; the sunken sluices strangled and shook deep down through the whirlpools sucking at their mouths; the flocks of scattered sea-birds—ducks and brant—veered into sight, dashed down toward the white waters or drove over with mad speed, while the winds screamed and the sky hung black like a torn and flapping sail.

And I, too, would have to drop upon all fours, with the mice and muskrats, and cling to the bank for my life, as the snarling river, leaping at me, would plunge clear over into the meadow below.

A winter blizzard is more deadly, but not more fearful, nor so wild and tumultuous. For in such a storm as this the foundations of the deep seem to be broken up, the frame of the world shaken, and you, and the mice, and the muskrats, share alike the wild, fierce spirit and the fear.

To be out in such a storm, out where you can feel its full fury, as upon a strip of bank in the midst of the churning waters, is good for one. To experience a common peril with your fellow mortals, though they be only mice and muskrats, is good for one; for it is to share by so much in their humble lives, and by so much to live outside of one's own little self.

And then again, we are so accustomed to the order and fair weather of our part of the globe, that we get to feel as if the universe were being particularly managed for us; nay, that we, personally, are managing the universe. To flatten out on a quaking ridge of earth or be blown into the river; to hear no voice but the roar of the storm, and to have no part or power in the mighty tumult of such a storm, makes one feel about the size of a mouse, makes one feel how vast is the universe, and how fearful the vortex of its warring forces!

The shriek of those winds is still in my ears, the sting of the driving rains still on my face, the motion of that frail mud bank, swimming like a long sea-serpent in the swirling waters, I can still feel to my finger-tips. And the growl of the river, the streaming shreds of the sky, the confusion beneath and about me, the mice and muskrats clinging with me for a foothold—I live it all again at the first spatter of a February rain upon my face.

To be out in a February freshet, out in a big spring break-up, is to get a breaking up one's self, a preparation, like Nature's, for a new lease of life—for spring.

CHAPTER XI

A BREACH IN THE BANK

THE February freshet had come. We had been expecting it, but no one along Maurice River had ever seen so wild and warm and ominous a spring storm as this. So sudden and complete a break-up of winter no one could remember; nor so high a tide, so rain-thick and driving a south wind. It had begun the night before, and now, along near noon, the river and meadows were a tumult of white waters, with the gale so strong that one could hardly hold his own on the drawbridge that groaned from pier to pier in the grip of the maddened storm.

It was into the teeth of this gale that a small boy dressed in large yellow "oil-skins" made his slow way out along the narrow bank of the river toward the sluices that controlled the tides of the great meadows.

The boy was *in* the large yellow oil-skins; not dressed, no, for he was simply inside of them, his feet and hands and the top of his head having managed to work their way out. It seems, at least, that his head was partly out, for on the top of the oil-skins sat a large black sou'wester. And in the arms of the oil-skins lay an old army musket, so big and long that it seemed to be walking away with the oil-skins, as the oil-skins seemed to be walking away with the boy.

I can feel the kick of that old musket yet, and the prick of the dried sand-burs among which she knocked me. I can hear the rough rasping of the chafing legs of those oil-skins too, though I was not the boy this time inside of them. But I knew the boy who was, a real boy; and I know that he made his careful way along the trembling river-bank out into the sunken meadows, meadows that later on I saw the river burst into and claim—and it still claims them, as I saw only last summer, when after thirty years of absence I once more stood at the end of that bank looking over a watery waste which was once the richest of farm lands.

Never, it seemed, had the village known such wind and rain and such a tide. It was a strange, wild scene from the drawbridge—wharves obliterated, river white with flying spume and tossing ice-cakes, the great bridge swaying and shrieking in the wind, and over everything the blur of the swirling rain.

The little figure in yellow oil-skins was not the only one that had gone along the bank since morning, for a party of men had carefully inspected every foot of the bank to the last sluice, for fear that there might be a weak spot somewhere. Let a breach occur with such a tide as this and it could never be stopped.

And now, somewhat past noon, the men were again upon the bank. As they neared Five-Forks sluice, the central and largest of the water-gates, they heard a smothered boom above the scream of the wind in their ears. They were startled; but it was only the sound of a gun somewhere off in the meadow. It was the gun of the boy in the oil-skins.

Late that afternoon Doctor "Sam," driving home along the flooded road of the low back swamp, caught sight, as he came out in view of the river, of a little figure in yellow oil-skins away out on the meadow.

As the mist and rain were fast mixing with the dusk of the twilight, he quickened his steps. His path in places was hardly a foot wide, covered with rose and elder bushes mostly, but bare in spots where holes and low worn stretches had been recently built up with cubes of the tough blue mud of the flats.

The tide was already even with the top of the bank and was still rising. It leaped and hit at his feet as he picked his way along. The cakes of white ice crunched and heeled up against the bank with here and there one flung fairly across his path. The tossing water frequently splashed across. Twice he jumped places where the tide was running over down into the meadows below.

How quickly the night had come! It was dark when he reached Five-Forks sluice—the middle point in the long, high bank. While still some distance off he heard the sullen roar of the big sluice, through which the swollen river was trying to force its way.

He paused to listen a moment. He knew the peculiar voice of every one of these gateways, as he knew every foot of the river-bank.

There was nothing wrong with the sullen roar. But how deep and threatening! He could *feel* the sound even better than he could hear it, far down below him. He started forward, to pass on, when he half felt, through the long, regular throbbing of the sluice, a shorter, faster, closer quiver, as of a small running stream in the bank very near his feet.

Dropping quickly to his knees, he laid his ear to the wet earth. A cold, black hand seemed to seize upon him. He heard the purr of running water!

It must be down about three feet. He could distinctly feel it tearing through.

Without rising he scrambled down the meadow side of the bank to see the size of the breach. He could hear nothing of it for the boiling at the gates of the sluice. It was so dark he could scarcely see. But near the bottom the mud suddenly caved beneath his feet, and a rush of cold water caught at his knees.

The hole was greater than he feared.

Crawling back to the top of the bank, he leaned out over the river side. A large cake of ice hung in water in front of him. He pushed it aside and, bending until his face barely cleared the surface of the river, he discovered a small sucking eddy, whose swirling hole he knew ran into the breach.

He edged farther out and reached down under the water and touched the upper rim of the hole. How large might it be? Swinging round, he dug his fingers into the bank and lowered himself feet first until he stood in the hole. It was the size of a small bucket, but he could almost feel it going beneath his feet, and a sudden terror took hold upon him.

He was only a boy, and the dark night, the wild river, the vast, sweeping storm, the roar and tremor and tumult flattened him for a moment to the ridge of the bank in a panic of fear!

But he heard the water running, he felt the bank going directly beneath where he lay, and getting to his feet he started for the village. A single hasty step and, but for the piles of the sluice, he would have plunged into the river.

He must feel his way; but he never could do it in time to save the bank. The breach must be stopped at once. He must stop it and keep it stopped until the next patrol brought help.

Feeling his way back, he dropped again upon

his hands and knees above the breach to think for a moment. The cake of ice hung as before in the eddy. Catching it, he tipped it and thrust it down across the mouth of the hole, but it slipped from his cold fingers and dived away. He pushed down the butt of his musket, turned it flat, but it was not broad enough to cover the opening. Then he lowered himself again, and stood in it, wedging the musket in between his boots; but he could feel the water still tearing through at the sides, and eating all the faster.

He clambered back to the top of the bank, put his hand to his mouth and shouted. The only answer was the scream of the wind and the cry of a brant passing overhead.

Then the boy laughed. "Easy enough," he muttered, and, picking up the musket, he leaned once more out over the river and thrust the steel barrel of the gun hard into the mud just below the hole. Then, stepping easily down, he sat squarely into the breach, the gun like a stake in front of him sticking up between his knees.

Then he laughed again, as he caught his breath, for he had squeezed into the hole like a stopper into a bottle, his big oil-skins filling the breach completely.

The water stood above the middle of his breast, and the tide was still rising. Darkness had now settled, but the ghostly ice-cakes, tipping, slipping toward him, were spectral white. He had to shove them back as now and then one rose before his face. The sky was black, and the deep water below him was blacker. And how cold it was!

Doctor Sam had been stopped by the flooded roads on his way home, and lights shone in the windows as he entered the village. He turned a little out of his way and halted in front of a small cottage near the bridge.

"Is Joe here?" he asked.

"No," answered the mother; "he went down the meadow for muskrats and has not returned yet. He's probably over with the men at the store."

Doctor Sam drove on to the store.

There was no boy in yellow oil-skins in the store.

Doctor Sam picked up a lighted lantern.

"Come on," he said; "I'm wet, but I want a look at those sluices," and started for the river, followed immediately by the men, whom he led in single file out along the bank.

Swinging his lantern low, he pushed into the teeth of the gale at a pace that left the line of lights straggling far behind.

"What a night!" he growled. "If I had a boy of my own—" and he threw the light as far as he could over the seething river and then down over the flooded meadow.

Ahead he heard the roar of Five-Forks sluice, and swung his lantern high, as if to signal it, so like the rush of a coming train was the sound of the waters.

But the little engineer in yellow oil-skins could not see the signal. He had almost ceased to watch. With his arm cramped about his gun, he was still at his post; but

119

the ice-cakes floated in and touched him; the water no longer felt cold.

On this side, then on that, out over the swollen river, down into the tossing meadow flared the lantern as the doctor worked his way along.

Above the great sluice he paused a moment, then bent his head to the wind and started on, when his foot touched something soft that yielded strangely, sending a shiver over him, and his light fell upon a bunch of four dead muskrats lying in the path.

Along the meadow side flashed the lantern, up and over the river side, and Doctor Sam, reaching quickly down, drew a limp little form in yellow oil-skins out of the water, as the men behind him came up.

A gurgle, a hiss, a small whirlpool sucking at the surface,—and the tide was again tearing through the breach that the boy had filled.

The men sprang quickly to their task, and did it well, while Doctor Sam, shielding the limp little form from the wind, forced a vial of something between the white lips, saying over to himself as he watched the closed eyes open, "If I had a boy of my own—If I had a boy—"

*   *   *   *   *   *

No, Doctor Sam never had a boy of his own; but he always felt, I think, that the boy of those yellow oil-skins was somehow pretty nearly his.

*   *   *   *   *   *

After a long, cold winter how I love the spatter on

DREW A LIMP LITLE FORM OUT OF THE WATER

my face of the first February rain! The little trout brook below me foams and sometimes overruns the road, and as its small noise ascends the hill, I can hear—the wind on a great river, the wash of waves against a narrow bank, and the muffled roar of quaking sluices as when a February freshet is on.

CHAPTER XII

A CHAPTER OF THINGS TO HEAR THIS WINTER

I

YOU should hear the three great silences of winter: the wide, sudden silence that falls at twilight on the coming of the first winter frost; the smothered hush that waits the breaking of a winter storm; the crystal stillness, the speech of the stars, that pervades earth and sky on a brilliant, stirless winter night. You should hear—or is it feel?— them all.[52]

II

So should you hear the great voices of the winter: the voice of the north wind; the voice of a pine forest; the voice of the surf on a stormy shore. There is no music that I know like the wild mighty music of the winter winds in the winter woods. It will often happen

---

[52]It is the stilling of the insects that makes for the first of these silences; the hushing of the winds the second; the magic touch of the cold the third.

that you can pass through a bare stretch of naked hardwoods immediately into a grove of thick-limbed spruces or pines. Never miss such an opportunity. Do not let the high winds of this winter blow on and away without your hearing them—at least once—as they sweep through the hardwoods on into the deep resounding pines.[53]

III

Did you ever hear the running, rumbling, reverberating sound of the shore-to-shore split of a wide sheet of new ice? You will hear it as the sun rises over the pond, as the tide turns in the ice-bound river, and when the ice contracts with falling temperature,—a startling bolt of sound, a quake, that cleaves the ice across and splits its way into the heart of the frozen hills.[54]

IV

One of the most unnatural of all the sounds out-of-doors is the clashing, glassy rattle of trees ice-coated and shaken by the wind. It is as if you were in some weird china shop, where the curtains, the very clothes of the customers, were all of broken glass. It is the rattle of death, not of life; no, rather it is the rustle of the ermine

[53]The voice of the great spring storm should be added to these, and the shriek of the wind about the house.

[54]You should not only hear, but you should also feel this split—passing with a thrilling shock beneath your feet.

robe of Winter, as he passes crystal-booted down his crystal halls.

V

If winter is the season of large sounds, it is also the season of small sounds, for it is the season of wide silence when the slightest of stirrings can be heard. Three of these small sounds you must listen for this winter: the smothered *tinkle-tunkle* of water running under thin ice, as where the brook passes a pebbly shallow; then the *tick-tick-tick* of the first snowflakes hitting the brown leaves on a forest floor; then the fine sharp scratch of a curled and toothed beech leaf skating before a noiseless breath of wind over the crusty snow. Only he that hath ears will hear these sounds, speaking, as they do, for the vast voiceless moments of the winter world.[55]

VI

I have not heard the "covey call" of the quail this winter. But there is not a quail left alive in all the fields and sprout-lands within sound of me. I used to hear them here on Mullein Hill; a covey used to roost down the wooded hillside in front of the house; but even they are gone—hunted out of life; shot and eaten off of

[55]How many other of the small voices do you know? The chirp of the kinglets; the scratching of mice in a shock of corn; the—but you write a story about them. So listen for yourself.

my small world. What a horribly hungry animal man is![56]

But you may have the quail still in your fields. If so, then go out toward dusk on a quiet, snowy day, especially if you have heard shooting in the fields that day, and try to hear some one of the covey calling the flock together: *Whir-r-rl-ee! Whir-r-rl-ee! Whirl-ee-gee!*—the sweetest, softest, tenderest call you will ever hear!

VII

And you certainly do have chickadees in your woods. If so, then go out any time of day, but go on a cold, bleak, blustery day, when everything is a-shiver, and, as Uncle Remus would say, "meet up" with a chickadee. It is worth having a winter, just to meet a chickadee in the empty woods and hear him call—a little pin-point of live sound, an undaunted, unnumbed voice interrupting the thick jargon of the winter to tell you that all this bluster and blow and biting cold can't get at the heart of a bird that must weigh, all told, with all his winter feathers on, fully—an ounce or two!

VIII

And then the partridge—you must hear him, bursting like a bottled hurricane from the brown leaves at your feet![57]

[56]Do all you can to preserve the quail. Don't shoot.

[57]Along toward spring you should hear him "drumming" for a mate—a rapid motion of his wings much like the hollow sound of a distant drum.

ONE OF THE COVEY CALLING THE FLOCK TOGETHER

IX

Among the sweet winter sounds, that are as good to listen to as the songs of the summer birds, you should hear: the loud joyous cackling of the hens on a sunny January day; the munching of horses at night when the wild winds are whistling about the barn; the quiet hum about the hives,—

"When come the calm mild days, as still such days will come,
To call the squirrel and the bee from out their winter home."

And then, the sound of the first rain on the shingles— the first February rain after a long frozen period! How it spatters the shingles with *spring—spring—spring!*

X

It was in the latter end of December, upon a gloomy day that was heavy with the oppression of a coming storm. In the heart of the maple swamp all was still and cold and dead. Suddenly, as out of a tomb, I heard the small, thin cry of a tiny tree-frog. And how small and thin it sounded in the vast silences of that winter swamp! And yet how clear and ringing! A thrill of life tingling out through the numb, nerveless body of the woods that has ever since made a dead day for me impossible.

Have you heard him yet?

XI

"After all," says some one of our writers, "it is only a matter of which side of the tree you stand on, whether it is summer or winter." Just so. But, after all, is it not a good thing to stand on the winter side during the winter? to have a winter while we have it, and then have spring? No shivering around on the spring side of the tree for me. I will button up my coat, brace my back against the winter side and shout to the hoary old monarch—

> "And there's a hand, my trusty fiere,
> And gie's a hand o' thine;"

and what a grip he has!

CHAPTER XIII

THE LAST DAY OF WINTER

ACCORDING to the almanac March 21st is the last day of winter. The almanac is not always to be trusted—not for hay weather, or picnic weather, or sailing weather; but you can always trust it for March 21st weather. Whatever the weather man at Washington predicts about it, whatever comes,—snow, sleet, slush, rain, wind, or frogs and sunshine,—March 21st is the last day of winter.[58]

The sun "crosses the line" that day; spring crosses with him; and I cross over with the spring.

Let it snow! I have had winter enough. Let the wind rage! It cannot turn back the sun; it cannot blow away the "equinoctial line"; it cannot snow under my determination to have done, here and now, with winter!

The sun crosses to my side of the Equator on the 21st of March; there is nothing in the universe that can stop him. I cross over the line with him; and there is nothing under the sun that can stop me. When you

[58]Get an almanac and study the old weather signs.

want it to be spring, if you have the sun on your side of the line you can have spring. Hitching your wagon to a star is a very great help in getting along; but having the big sun behind you—

"When descends on the Atlantic
The gigantic
Storm-wind of the equinox"[59]

is a tremendous help in ridding you of a slow and, by this time, wearisome winter, storm-wind and all.

Almanacs are not much to trust in; but if ever you prize one, it is on the 21st of March,—that is, if you chance to live in New England. Yet you can get along without the almanac—even in New England. Hang it up under the corner of the kitchen mantelpiece and come out with me into the March mud. We are going to find the signs of spring, the proofs that this is the last day of winter, that the sun is somewhere in the heavens and on this side of the equatorial line.

Almanac or no, and with all other signs snowed under, there are still our bones! Spring is in our bones. I cannot tell you how it gets into them, nor describe precisely how it feels. But, then, I do not need to. For you feel it in your bones too—a light, hollow feeling, as if your bones were birds' bones, and as if you could flap your arms and fly!

Only that you feel it more in your feet; and you will start and run, like the Jungle-folk, like Mowgli—run, run, run! Oh, it is good to have bones in your body,

---

[59] *"When descends on the Atlantic"*: from Longfellow's "Seaweed."

young bones with the "spring-running," in their joints, instead of the grit of rheumatism to stiffen and cripple you!

The roads are barely thawed. The raw wind is penetrating, and we need our greatcoats to keep out the cold. But look! A flock of robins—twenty of them,

dashing into the cedars, their brown breasts glowing warm and red against the dull sky and the dark green of the trees! And wait—before we go down the hill—here behind the barn—no, there he dives from the telephone wire—Phœbe! He has just gotten back, and is simply killing time now (and insects too), waiting for Mrs. Phœbe to arrive, and housekeeping to begin.

Don't move! There in the gray clouds—two soaring, circling hen-hawks! *Kee-ee-you! Kee-ee-you!* Round and round they go, their shrill, wild whistle piercing the four quarters of the sky and tingling down the cold spine of every forest tree and sapling, stirring their life blood until it seems to run red into their tops.

For see the maple swamp off yonder—the ashy gray of the boles, a cold steel-color two thirds of the way toward the top, but there changing into a faint garnet, a flush of warmth and life that seems almost to have come since morning!

Let us go on now, for I want to get some watercress from the brook—the first green growing thing for the table thus far!—and some pussy-willows for the same table, only not to eat. (There are many good things in this world that are not good to eat.)

If the sun were shining I should take you by way of the beehives to show you, dropping down before their open doors, a few eager bees bringing home baskets of pollen from the catkins of the hazelnut bushes.

The hazelnut bushes are in bloom! Yes, in bloom! No, the skunk-cabbages are not out yet, nor the hepaticas, nor the arbutus; but the hazelnut bushes are in bloom, and—see here, under the rye straw that covers the strawberry-bed—a small spreading weed, green, and cheerily starred with tiny white flowers!

It is the 21st of March; the sun has crossed the line; the phoebes have returned; and here under the straw in the garden the chick-weed—*starwort*,—first of the flowers, is in blossom!

But come on; I am not going back yet. This is the last day of winter. Cold? Yes, it is cold, raw, wretched, gloomy, with snow still in the woods, with frost still in the ground, and with not a frog or hyla[60] anywhere to be heard. But come along. This is the last day of winter—of winter? No, no, it is the first day of spring. Robins back, phœbes back, watercress for the table, chickweed in blossom, and a bird's nest with eggs in it! Winter? Spring? Birds' eggs, did I say?

The almanac is mixed again. It always is. Who's Who in the Seasons when all of this is happening on the 21st of March? For here is the bird's nest with eggs in it, just as I said.

Watch the hole up under that stub of a limb while I tap on the trunk. How sound asleep! But I will wake them. *Rap-rap-rap!* There he comes—the big barred owl!

[60]*frog or hyla:* The hylas belong to the family Hylidæ and include our tree-toad, and our little tree-frog.

134

Climb up and take a peek at the eggs, but don't you dare to touch them! Of course you will not. I need not have been so quick and severe in my command; for, if we of this generation do not know as much about some things as our fathers knew, we do at least know better than they that the owls are among our best friends and are to be most jealously protected.

Climb up, I say, and take a peek at those round white eggs, and tell me, Is it spring or winter? Is it the last day, or the first day, or the first and last in one? What a high mix-up is the weather—especially this New England sort!

But look at that! A snowflake! Yes, it is beginning to snow—with the sun crossing the line! It is beginning to snow, and down with the first flakes, like a bit of summer sky drops a bluebird, calling softly, sweetly, with notes that melt warm as sunshine into our hearts.

"For, lo, the winter is past,[61] the rain is over and gone." But see how it snows! Yes, but see—

> The willows gleam with silver light;
> The maples crimson glow—
> The first faint streaks on winter's east,
> Far-off and low.
>
> The northward geese, with wingèd wedge,
> Have split the frozen skies,
> And called the way for weaker wings,
> Where midnight lies.

[61] *"For, lo, the winter is past"*: from The Song of Songs, or The Song of Solomon, in the Bible.

To-day a warm wind wakes the marsh;
    I hear the hylas peep
And o'er the pebbly ford, unbound,
    The waters leap.

The lambs bleat from the sheltered folds;
    Low whispers spread the hills:
The rustle of the spring's soft robes
    The forest fills.

The night, ah me! fierce flies the storm
    Across the dark dead wold;
The swift snow swirls; and silence falls
    On stream and fold.

All white and still lie stream and hill—
    The winter dread and drear!
Then from the skies a bluebird flies
    And—spring is here!

NOTES AND SUGGESTIONS TO THE TEACHER

INTRODUCTION

AS in *The Fall of the Year*, so here in *Winter*, the second volume of this series, I have tried by story and sketch and suggestion to catch the spirit of the season. In this volume it is the large, free, strong, fierce, wild soul of Winter which I would catch, the bitter boreal might that, out of doors, drives all before it; that challenges all that is wild and fierce and strong and free and large within us, till the bounding red blood belts us like an equator, and the glow of all the tropics blooms upon our faces and down into the inmost of our beings.

Winter within us means vitality and purpose and throbbing life; and without us in our fields and woods it means widened prospect, the storm of battle, the holiness of peace, the poetry of silence and darkness and emptiness and death. And I have tried throughout this volume to show that Winter is only a symbol, that death is only an appearance, that life is everywhere, and that everywhere life dominates even while it lies buried under the winding-sheet of the snow.

> "A simple child,
> That lightly draws its breath,
> What should it know of death?"

Why, this at least, that the winter world is not dead; that the cold is powerless to destroy; that life flees and hides and sleeps, only to waken again, forever stronger than death—fresher, fairer, sweeter for its long winter rest.

But first of all, and always, I have tried here to be a naturalist and nature-lover, pointing out the sounds and sights, the things to do, the places to visit, the how and why, that the children may know the wild life of winter, and through that knowledge come to love winter for its own sake.

And they will love it. Winter seems to have been made especially for children. They do not have rheumatism. Let the old people hurry off down South, but turn the children loose in the snow. The sight of a snowstorm affects a child as the smell of catnip affects a cat. He wants to roll over and over and over in it. And he should roll in it; the snow is his element as it is a polar bear cub's.

I love the winter, and so do all children—its bare fields, empty woods, flattened meadows, its ranging landscapes, its stirless silences, its tumult of storms, its crystal nights with stars new cut in the glittering sky, its challenge, defiance, and mighty wrath. I love its wild life—its birds and animals; the shifts they make to conquer death. And then, out of this winter watching, I love the gentleness that comes, the sympathy, the understanding! One gets very close to the heart of Nature through such understanding.

CHAPTER I

HUNTING THE SNOW

"It must be a lovely place in the summer!" the dull and irritating often say to me, referring to my home in the country. What they mean is, of course, "How wretched a place the country is in winter!" But that attitude toward winter grows less and less common. We are learning how to enjoy the winter; and it is my hope that this volume may distinctly contribute to the knowledge that makes for that joy. Behind such joy is love, and behind the love is understanding, and behind the understanding is knowledge.

The trouble with those who say they hate winter is a lack of knowledge. They do not know the winter; they never tramp the woods and fields in winter; they have no calendar of the rare, the high-festival days of winter.

Such a day is the one of this opening chapter—"Hunting the Snow." And the winter is full of them; as full as the summer, I had almost said! The possibilities of winter for nature-study, for tramps afield, for outdoor sport—for joy and health and knowledge and poetry are quite as good as those of summer. Try it this winter. Indeed, let the coldest, dullest, deadest day this winter challenge you to discover to yourself and to your pupils some sight, some sound, some happening, or some thought of the world outside that shall add to their small understanding, or touch their ready imaginations, or awaken their eager love for Nature.

And do not let the rarer winter days pass (such as the day that follows the first snow-fall) without your taking them or sending them a-hunting the snow, else you will fail in duty as grievously as you would if you allowed a child to finish his public-school education without hearing of Bunker Hill.

In reading this first chapter lay emphasis upon: (1) the real excitement possible without a gun in such a hunt; (2) the keener, higher kind of joy in watching a live animal than in killing it; (3) the unfairness of hunting to kill; (4) the rapid extinction of our wild animals, largely caused by guns; (5) the necessity now for protection—for every pupil's doing all he can to protect wild life everywhere.

CHAPTER II

THE TURKEY DRIVE

This herding and driving of turkeys to market is common in other sections of the country, particularly in Kentucky. I have told the story (as told to me by one who saw the flock) in order to bring out the force of instinct and habit, and the unreasoning nature of the animal mind as compared with man's.

CHAPTER III

WHITE-FOOT

There is a three-pronged point to this chapter: (1) the empty birds' nests are not things to mourn over. The birds are safe and warm down south; and they will build fresh, clean nests when they get back. Teach your children to see things as they are—the wholesomeness, naturalness, wisdom, and poetry of Nature's arrangement. The poets are often sentimental; and most sentimentality is entirely misplaced. (2) The nest abandoned by the bird may be taken up by the mouse. The deadest, commonest of things may prove full of life and interest upon close observation. Summer may go; but winter comes and brings its own interests and rewards. So does youth go and old age come. There is nothing really abandoned in nature—nothing utterly lacking interest. (3) A mouse is not a Bengal tiger; but he is a whole mouse and in the completeness of his life just as large and interesting as the tiger. If the small, the common, the things right at hand, are not interesting, it is not their fault—not the mouse's fault—but ours.

CHAPTER IV

THINGS TO SEE THIS WINTER

If you have at hand *The Fall of the Year*, read again the suggestions in the chapter on "Things To See This

Fall," making use of this chapter as you did of that (1) as the object of a field excursion—or of several excursions until all the things suggested here have been seen; (2) as a test of the pupil's actual study of nature; for there is scarcely a city child who cannot get far enough into nature (though he get no farther than the city park), and often enough to see most of the things pointed out in this chapter; (3) as suggestions for further study and observation by the pupils—things that they have seen which might be added to these ten here, and written about for composition work in English.

CHAPTER V

CHRISTMAS IN THE WOODS

Let this chapter be read very close to the Christmas recess, when your children's minds are full of Christmas thoughts. This unconventional turn to the woods, this thought of Christmas among the animals and birds, might easily be the means of awakening many to an understanding of the deeper, spiritual side of nature-study—that we find in Nature only what we take to her; that we get back only what we give. It will be easy for them to take the spirit of Christmas into the woods because they are so full of it; and so it will be easy for them to feel the woods giving it back to them—the very last and best reward of nature-study. No, don't be afraid that they are incapable of such lessons, of such thoughts and emotions. Some few may be; but no teacher ever yet erred by too much faith in the capacity of her pupils for the higher, deeper things.

CHAPTER VI

CHICKADEE

Read to the pupils Emerson's poem "The Titmouse," dwelling on the lines,—

> "Here was this atom in full breath,
> Hurling defiance at vast death," etc.

and the part beginning,—

> "'Tis good will makes intelligence,"

letting the students learn by heart the chickadee's little song,—

> "Live out of doors
> In the great woods, on prairie floors," etc.

Poem and chapter ought mutually to help each other. Read the chapter slowly, explaining clearly as you go on, making it finally plain that this mere "atom" of life is greater than all the winter death, no matter how "vast."

CHAPTER VII

THINGS TO DO THIS WINTER

Make a point of going into the winter woods and fields, taking the pupils as often as possible with you. It may be impossible for your city children to get the rare chance of glare ice; but don't miss it if it comes.

This is the time to start your bird-study; to awaken

sympathy and responsibility in your pupils by teaching them to feed the birds; to cultivate cheerfulness and the love of "hardness" in them by breasting with them a bitter winter gale for the pure joy of it. Use the suggestions here for whatever of resourcefulness and hardiness you can cultivate in the girls as well as in the boys.

CHAPTER VIII

THE MISSING TOOTH

I believe this to be one of the most important chapters in the volume, dark and terrible as its lesson may appear. But grim, dark death itself is not so dark as fear of the truth. If you teach nothing else, by precept and example, teach love for the truth—for the whole truth in nature as everywhere else. Winter is a fact; let us face it. Death is a fact; let us face it; and by facing it half of its terror will disappear; nay more, for something of its deep reasonableness and meaning will begin to appear, and we shall be no more afraid. The *all* of this is beyond a child, as it is beyond us; but the habit of looking honestly and fearlessly at things must be part of a child's education, as later on it must be the very sum of it.

Great tact and fine feeling must be exercised if you happen to have among the scholars one of the handicapped—one lacking any part, as the muskrat lacked—lest the application be taken personally. But let the lesson be driven home: the need every boy and girl has for a strong, full-membered body,—even for every one of his teeth,—if he is to live at his physical best.

CHAPTER IX

THE PECULIAR 'POSSUM

Make this chapter, as far as you can, the one in the volume for most intensive study. Show the pupils how the study of animal life is connected with geology, tell them of the record of life in the fossils of the rocks, the kinds of strange beasts that once inhabited the earth. Show them again how the study of animals in their anatomy is not the study of one—say of man, but how man and all the mammals, the reptiles, the birds, the fishes, the insects, on and on back to the single-celled amœba, are all related to each other, all links in one long wonder chain of life.

CHAPTER X

A FEBRUARY FRESHET

This chapter and the next go together—this for the lover of wild life, the next for the lover of adventure. The spring freshet is one of the most interesting of the year of days for animal study—better even than the day after the first snowfall. But more than this, let both chapters suggest to you how primitive and elemental the real world is after all; with what cataclysmal forces the seasons are changed. As summer often passes into autumn with a silencing frost that rests like a hush of awe over the land; so winter often gives way to spring with a rush of wind and tidal powers that seem to shake the foundations of the world. To feel these forces, to be a part of all these moods, to share in all these feelings— this, too, is one of the ends of nature-study.

CHAPTER XII

THINGS TO HEAR THIS WINTER

I should like to repeat here the suggestions in *The Fall of the Year* for this corresponding chapter. I will repeat only: "that you are the teacher, not the book. The book is but a suggestion. You begin where it leaves off; you fill out where it is lacking." For these are not all the sounds of winter; indeed they may not be the characteristic sounds in your neighborhood. No matter: the lesson is not this or that sound, but that your pupils learn to listen for sounds, for the voices of the season, whatever those voices may be in their own particular region. The trouble is that we have ears, and literally hear not, eyes and see not, souls and feel not. Teach your pupils to use their eyes, ears, yes and hearts, and all things else will be added unto them in the way of education.

CHAPTER XIII

THE LAST DAY OF WINTER

Do all that you can to teach the signs of the zodiac, the days of the seasons, and all the doings of the astronomical year. All that old lore of the skies is in danger of being lost. Some readers will say: "The author is not consistent! He loves the winter and here he is impatient to be done with it!" Some explanation on your part may be necessary: that the call of the spring is the call of life, a call so loud and strong that all life—human and wild, animal and vegetable,—hears it and is impatient to obey. If possible take your scholars upon a walk at this raw edge of the season when they will feel the chill but also the stirring of life all about them.

CPSIA information can be obtained
at www.ICGtesting.com
Printed in the USA
BVHW071314180421
605249BV00022B/533